Making the Principal TExES Exam Real

Making the Principal TExES Exam Real

Competency-Based Case Studies
With Practice Questions

Elaine L. Wilmore

CORWIN
A SAGE Company

FOR INFORMATION:

Corwin
A SAGE Company
2455 Teller Road
Thousand Oaks, California 91320
(800) 233-9936
www.corwin.com

SAGE Publications Ltd.
1 Oliver's Yard
55 City Road
London EC1Y 1SP
United Kingdom

SAGE Publications India Pvt. Ltd.
B 1/I 1 Mohan Cooperative Industrial Area
Mathura Road, New Delhi 110 044
India

SAGE Publications Asia-Pacific Pte. Ltd.
3 Church Street
#10-04 Samsung Hub
Singapore 049483

Executive Editor: Arnis Burvikovs
Associate Editor: Desirée A. Bartlett
Editorial Assistant: Andrew Olson
Production Editor: Amy Schroller
Copy Editor: Michelle Ponce
Typesetter: C&M Digitals (P) Ltd.
Proofreader: Rae-Ann Goodwin
Indexer: Sylvia Coates
Cover Designer: Anupama Krishnan
Marketing Manager: Lisa Lysne

Copyright © 2015 by Corwin

Printed in the United States of America

A catalog record of this book is available from the Library of Congress.

ISBN 978-1-4833-6673-9

This book is printed on acid-free paper.

SFI® Certified Sourcing
www.sfiprogram.org
SFI-00453

15 16 17 18 19 10 9 8 7 6 5 4 3 2 1

Contents

Preface

*M*aking the Principal TExES Exam Real: Competency-Based Case Studies *With Practice Questions* was written to help Texas educators pass the Principal (068) Texas Examinations of Educator Standards (TExES). It is to be used by students and teachers seeking to pass either of the examinations as well as by universities and alternative preparation programs across the state. It is based on the standards, domains, and competencies provided through Texas law (19 Texas Administrative Code Chapter 241.15) and developed by the Texas State Board for Educator Certification (SBEC). It is written based on the years of experience Dr. Wilmore has as a teacher, counselor, principal, professor, and school board member. Using those experiences, she is also a popular and inspiring TExES preparation seminar presenter at universities, regional service centers, and other training sites around the state. She speaks, consults, does assessments, and is the keynote speaker at multiple functions across the state, nation, and beyond.

The nature of the book is both broad and specific. Early it provides the philosophy and theoretical framework for success on the Principal TExES exam. It details the Texas domains, competencies, and philosophy on which the exam is constructed. Each of the nine competency chapters provides case studies that are directly aligned to each of the competencies, has open-ended higher order thinking skills questions for discussion, and practice decision set questions with answers that are directly aligned with that competency. All are done in a down-to-earth, interesting manner while engaging the reader and connecting theory to practice.

Making the Principal TExES Exam Real: Competency-Based Case Studies With Practice Questions is also a tremendous asset for current administrators seeking to refine, refocus, or further develop their learner-centered leadership skills. It follows the same format and has the same voice as Dr. Wilmore's other highly successful Corwin TExES exam books:

- *Passing the Principal TExES Exam: Keys to Certification and School Leadership* (2nd ed.)
- *Passing the Superintendent TExES Exam: Keys to Certification and District Leadership*
- *Passing the PPR TExES Exam: Keys to Certification and Ethical Teaching* (With Amy Burkman)
- *Passing the Special Education TExES Exam: Keys to Certification and Exceptional Learners*
- *Passing the Supplemental ESL TExES Exam: Keys to Certification and English Language Learners*

With the author's proven record of success in TExES exam preparation, this book not only provides a solid theoretical framework for teaching ESL it also makes learning fun and inspires greatness. Readers will enjoy the book, be ready to pass the TExES Exam, and then to change the world—one campus at a time.

Acknowledgments

God has blessed me with such a wonderful family and so many great friends. It is simply impossible to acknowledge all of them for everything they have brought to my life. My books come from my heart and my faith as a gift to others. Without my family, friends, and my faith, where would my heart be? What would it hold?

So, in the simplest of words, thank you. Thank you to my husband, Greg, to our children Brandon and Brooke Wilmore, Brittani and Ryan Rollen, and our beautiful and brilliant grandchildren, Blair Elaine and Lucas Ryan. Thank you to my friends that always surround me with love and support. It would be absolutely impossible to name all of you, but here are but a few: Barbara Webb, Patti Dahlstrom, Brenda Wilmore Arrington, Sarah, Ben, Matt, Sam, Zach, Ella, Jeff, T. N., Larry and Diane Wilmore, Sophie and Tony Sarda, Marlene and Bill Carter, Wanda and John Rollen, Billie Westbrook, Helen and Wes Nelson, Dr. Joe and Kathy Martin, JoNell and Larry Jones, Betsy Ruffin, Brenda and Gregg Gammon, Dr. Bob and Becky Shaw, Dr. Linda and Ron Townzen, Dr. Wade, Renea, and Emily Smith, Dr. Mary Lynn Crow, Bob and Sallie Feavel, and my lifelong beloved childhood friends, Melda Cole Ward, Charlotte Dyson Vanett, and Kerry Van Doren Pedigo. And, last but certainly not least, I must also thank my gracious and diligent graduate assistant, Rachel McCarty-George, for helping me beyond measure.

Few are blessed with the quality and quantity of my family and friends.

Last, I must always thank my parents, the late Lee and Irene Litchfield, to whom I owe all that I am or ever will be. They taught me values, faith, a sense of humor, and to love and care for others. They also always supported my lifelong love of reading, libraries, and all things related to books. I miss you both so much. We will be together again someday too . . . in Heaven.

Love Always,
Elaine

. . . saying, I am Alpha and Omega, the first and the last: and,

what thou seest, write in a book . . .

Revelation 1:11

Publisher's Acknowledgments

Corwin gratefully acknowledges the contributions of the following reviewers:

Susan Bolte
Elementary School Principal
Providence Elementary
Aubrey, TX

Dalane E. Bouillion
Chief Academic Officer
Spring Independent
    School District
Houston, TX

William Allan Kritsonis
Professor, Dept. of
    Educational Leadership
University of Texas of the
    Permian Basin
Odessa, TX

Charles Lowery
Assistant Professor,
    Educational Administration
Ohio University
Athens, OH

About the Author

 Dr. Elaine Wilmore was a public school teacher, counselor, and elementary and middle school principal before she moved to higher education. She has extensive background in everything from early childhood education to creating and leading doctoral programs. She currently serves as ad interim chair of Education Leadership at Texas A&M University Texarkana. She formerly served as a professor, the chair of Educational Leadership, Counseling, and Foundations at Texas A&M Commerce, and as the founding doctoral director at the University of Texas of the Permian Basin. She also served at Dallas Baptist University as assistant vice president for educational networking and program director for the MEd and, again, the implementing director of the Doctor of Education degree in educational leadership.

Prior to her position at Dallas Baptist University, Dr. Wilmore served as special assistant to the dean for NCATE Accreditation, chair and associate professor of educational leadership and policy studies at the University of Texas at Arlington (UTA), and was the founder of all initial educational leadership graduate programs at UTA including the innovative field-based and grant-funded Educational Leadership UTA, which received national acclaim, and the Scholars of Practice program. While at UTA, she also served as director of university program development where she developed and was the original chair of the faculty governance committee for the College of Education. Dr. Wilmore's respect amongst those in higher education has led her to serve as a tenure reviewer in four states and a manuscript and proposal reviewer for many conferences and professional journals.

This book is dedicated with great love to my grandchildren,
Blair Elaine and Lucas Ryan, who are the joy of our hearts.
It is for them, and all other children, that we prepare great educators.

❧   ❧   ❧   ❧

Nehemiah said, "Go and enjoy choice food and sweet drinks,
and send some to those who have nothing prepared. This day is
holy to our Lord. Do not grieve, for the joy of the *Lord* is your strength.

Nehemiah 8:10, New International Version

❧   ❧   ❧   ❧

Now when Jesus saw the crowds, he went up on a mountainside and sat down. His disciples
came to him, and he began to teach them.

He said:

Blessed are the poor in spirit, for theirs is the kingdom of heaven.

Blessed are those who mourn, for they will be comforted.

Blessed are the meek, for they will inherit the earth

Blessed are those who hunger and thirst for righteousness, for they will be filled.

Blessed are the merciful, for they will be shown mercy

Blessed are the pure in heart, for they will see God.

Blessed are the peacemakers, for they will be called children of God.

Blessed are those who are persecuted because of righteousness, for theirs is the kingdom
of heaven.

Blessed are you when people insult you, persecute you and falsely say all kinds of evil
against you because of me. Rejoice and be glad, because great is your reward in heaven, for
in the same way they persecuted the prophets who were before you.

Matthew 5:1–13, New International Version

SECTION I

KNOWLEDGE, SKILLS, AND DISPOSITIONS

1

Hello!

Welcome to *Making the Principal TExES Exam Real: Competency-Based Case Studies With Practice Questions*. This book will be different from my *Passing the Principal TExES Exam: Keys to Certification and School Leadership* (2nd ed.) although it is built on the same competencies and theoretical framework.

Whereas the first book is designed strictly to teach you the theoretical framework of the test, this book will show you that framework in real life. Every competency from every domain has three case studies that directly address it. This will help you take the theory of the competency and see it in real life terms through the case studies—exactly like the 068 Principal TExES Exam does with the decision sets.

With three case studies for each of the nine competencies you have 27 case studies in this book. For each of them you will have reflective higher order thinking skills questions that can be used for individual study, but, even better, for use in class discussions so you can really wrap your mind around the case study and how it applies to that specific competency. There are five questions for each of the 27 case studies for a total of 135 higher order thinking skills questions.

Last, each chapter ends with five competency-based questions, for that specific competency, that are designed as practice questions for the actual TExES Exam. The answers are provided. Therefore, you will have 45 practice questions for the principal TExES Exam with five for each of the nine competencies.

All in all, *Making the Principal TExES Exam Real: Competency-Based Studies With Practice Questions* may be the best investment you make as you prepare for the Principal TExES Exam, outside of *Passing the Principal TExES Exam: Keys to Certification and School Leadership* (2nd ed.). My personal recommendation is that you read and study *Passing the Principal TExES Exam* first. Understand the theoretical framework. You need to comprehend the concepts around which the test is built in order to understand what the test developers are seeking from you in the questions.

Then purchase and thoroughly read and discuss this book. These two books, coupled with my brand new *Passing the Principal TExES Exam:*

Practice Tests for Success, should put you completely over the top of the TExES Exam. That is what we want. We want you to score so high they want to audit your test to see how you made such a high score in every domain.

So they are three different books with three different purposes. You want all of them. You want to read, study, and use all of them. They will do you no good sitting on a shelf.

Then when the day comes for you to test, you will knock the top out of it, one question at a time. Go for it!

2

What About All Those Domains and Competencies? They Scare Me

Overview of the TExES Learner-Centered Domains and Competencies

When preparing for this test, it is normal to be nervous. Being nervous equals being stressed. Remember that when you are stressed, your productivity goes down. In this instance, the productivity we are looking at is you passing the Principal TExES Exam. Therefore, as shown in Figure 2.1, our goal is to reduce your stress so your productivity will go up, not the other way around.

This test is built around 3 domains:

- School community leadership
- Instructional leadership
- Administrative leadership

Inside these three domains are nine competencies. They are not divided equally. There are three competencies in Domain I, four competencies in Domain II, and only two competencies in Domain III. The questions on the test are divided proportionately according to how many competencies per domain that there are. Because of that you can expect to see more questions

Figure 2.1 When Stress Goes Up, Productivity Goes Down

from Domain II, with four competencies, than you will see in Domain III with only two competencies. However, remember that all nine of the competencies are important, and all nine are covered on the test.

Regardless of which competency or domain we are addressing during our chat sessions, it is critically important to remember one thing. Figure 2.2 shows how all of the domains and competencies focus on the student and helping the student to be successful. Whatever modifications or adaptations

Figure 2.2 The Nine Domain Competencies Focus on Student Success

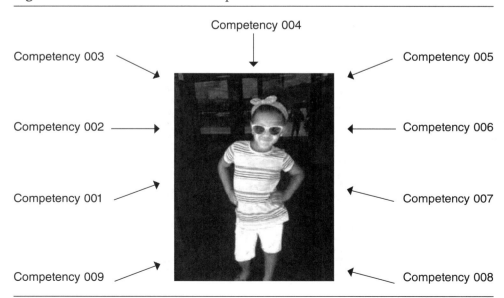

to Responses to Interventions (RtI) that are necessary for each student to be successful, must be done.

THE IDEAL SCENARIO

This test is built on what an ideal principal would do to create an ideal school. It is not based on what you see being done every day unless what you see being done is ideal. Therefore, if you pick an answer because it is something that seems would reasonably be done at your school, unless it is the *ideal* answer, you just picked the wrong answer. This test is not based on reality. It is based on what is ideal. How can we create ideal schools where all students are successful? How can you as principal create and lead these schools? That's the bottom line of this test.

Therefore, the ideal principal will always focus on the students and what is best for them rather than what is easiest or "the way we have always done it." Ideal principals use effective leadership strategies to lead their teachers to use the best research-based effective instructional strategies available for all students so that they can be successful. If a student is not successful, we modify what we are doing to help him or her. It is our job to teach all children, even if they are difficult to teach. It is our job to modify our teaching styles to meet their learning needs instead of the students' job to change their learning styles to meet our teaching styles. As principal, actions speak louder than words. We must model this as we deal with teachers, staff, and the entire school community.

THE CAMPUS VISION AND STRATEGIC GOAL SETTING

Figure 2.3 All Campus and Department Goals Should Be Student Focused

Mission = To move from reality to the vision.

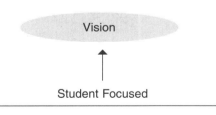

Student Focused

I cannot emphasize enough the significance of the campus vision—first that one actually exists and thereafter, that strategic plans are in place to see to ensure that it is achieved. Figure 2.3 shows how this is done.

To achieve this, use collaborative planning and data-based goal setting. *Every goal must be measurable and have a deadline, and you must identify (or acquire) the resources needed to meet it.* Without each of these things, it is not a goal. It is a dream. We do not have time to dream about success for every child. We do not have the political gravitas to hope that all students will do well on the State of Texas Assessments of Academic Readiness (STARR) or other exams. Hoping is not a plan. Looking at multiple sources of data gives you the resources to set reasonable, measureable goals that can and should be reached. Continuous assessment should be taking place to guarantee progress is being made toward each goal. If not, why not? If something is not working, change it. If the horse is dead, get off. If we have a goal of improving attendance by X%, we know via continuous assessment whether we are on track to meet it. If we are not, it is time to modify and adjust our strategies. In other words, we must do something different to make sure we do increase attendance by X%.

In order to develop a vision, we must first know where we are. What is our school's reality? How do we know this? We know this by looking at our data, by looking at lots and lots of data. We do this by using the Elaine Wilmore 1–2–3–4 Plan, shown in Figure 2.4 and discussed in detail later.

Figure 2.4   The 1–2–3–4 Plan

1. Develop, Create
2. Articulate, Communicate
3. Implement, Just Do It
4. Steward, Evaluate

We do this by talking to teachers, staff, and other members of the school community to get their perceptions of the strengths and weaknesses of the campus as well as how to improve them. Once we know where we are, our reality, together we collaboratively determine where we want to be. Where we want to be is our vision. The ministeps to get to the vision are our goals. The things we will do to get to our goals are our strategies. All are important in moving us from where we are, our reality, to where we want to be, our vision. This includes diagnosing organizational health and moral vision also as shown in Figure 2.5.

Let's do an example. Let's say we want to improve the attendance of Hispanic males (being specific) at our school. We can't just *say* we want to improve the attendance of Hispanic males. We have to take action.

First, we must set a measureable goal with a deadline. Remember, goals without deadlines are only dreams. So we could say, "We will increase the attendance rate of Hispanic male students by 3% during this academic year." In so doing, we are making the goal measureable (by 3%), and we are setting a deadline (this academic year).

But we are not finished. Thus far we are just talking. We are not taking action. We need action. Therefore, *exactly* how are we going to improve the attendance of Hispanic male students this year? Be specific. What exact strategies will your campus use to collaboratively improve attendance? These are the strategies we list under the goal of increasing attendance. They are specifically *aligned* to increasing attendance because that is their focus. If you cannot come up with any strategies,

Figure 2.5   Steps Must be Taken to Diagnose Organizational Health and Moral Vision

any activities, any plans for improving attendance, you do not have a goal. You have a dream. Dreams rarely come true without action.

And thus you build a campus improvement plan to take you from reality to the vision of the school

Do you get the picture? Each step feeds into the next to take us from where we are (reality) to ideal (our vision). During each step along the way, we keep our eyes on the students and what is best for them because, in the end, *it is all about the students*. After all, nothing else matters. We are a school. We are about students.

■ COMPETENCY-BASED PRINCIPALS: THE ELAINE WILMORE 1–2–3–4 PLAN

Competency–based principals are always visionaries, looking to the future. The Elaine Wilmore 1–2–3–4 Plan has already been referenced. Refer back to Figure 2.4 now. The plan addresses the future in four ways:

1. Developing (creating, planning) a campus vision

2. Articulating (telling, communicating) the campus vision so all stakeholders know, understand, and participate in it

3. Implementing (doing) the campus vision; putting it into action rather than just something on paper

4. Being good stewards (caregivers as well as evaluators) of the campus vision

This constitutes the Elaine Wilmore 1234 Plan which will help you with the questions that ask you what comes *first* or *initially*. It is based on these four steps. This plan is very important to your success as a principal and in your life. Remember the order: 1234. Think about how you could apply these same concepts in your daily life.

Everyone is necessary to achieve a student-focused campus vision. The competencies refer to the school community as including everyone short of the whole world. In truth, it includes the students themselves, their families or caregivers, all educators, including *you*, community members, churches, and civic resources. I emphasize the *you*, because people tend to think of so many things as other people's responsibilities or tasks, when in truth, these responsibilities belong to all of us. All of us together work to do everything necessary to promote a healthy and attainable/measureable campus vision that is focused on success for *all* students, not just the ones that are easy to teach.

The competencies talk about "diverse sociological, linguistic, cultural, and other factors" that could impact student learning as shown in Figure 2.6. In essence, this means everything. Everything that happens each day can impact the campus vision, thus, it impacts student learning. The same is true in reverse. Everything that impacts student learning has an obvious impact on the campus vision. The two are directly aligned.

Thus, societal factors do impact the campus, student learning, and the vision. Take 9/11 as an example. None of us got up that morning and

Figure 2.6   Diverse Sociological, Linguistic, and Cultural Factors Impact Learning

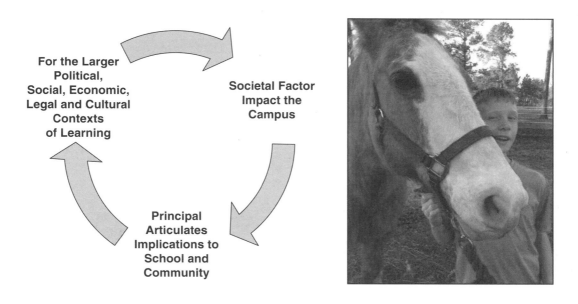

thought, "Oh, today is the day terrorists are going to attack America." Yet, they did. What they did had an impact on every school, town, and citizen in America. You never know what is going to happen, so you must always be prepared. Always be on full red alert, because, believe me, anything that can happen, will.

These societal factors mean principals must articulate their implications to the entire school community, which we have already learned means everyone. Why must this be done? It is done for the larger political, social, economic, legal, and cultural concepts of learning. If you do not think all of those are important, think back to 9/11.

Steps must be taken to diagnose the campus organizational health as well as the ethical and moral vision within the campus to maximize learning. We cannot simply assume that all is well. Frankly, we cannot even assume that everyone on the campus even gives a flip about the vision of the school. So, what are you, as the ideal principal, going to do about it?

ALIGNMENT ■

Much can be learned by simply talking to people and asking them their opinions on various topics. Open, collaborative faculty meetings where differences of opinions are respected, not challenged, will lead to a more open and inclusive vision. Also, there are many surveys and inventories to help identify areas of interest or need in a nonthreatening manner. In addition, the Region Service Centers are happy to help. Competency 003, which we will discuss shortly, focuses exclusively on the topic of a fair and ethical campus environment. As the leader, you must model the epitome of ethical leadership. You cannot just talk about it. Your words must match your actions. In the simplest of terms, your walk must match your talk. Your walk and talk must be aligned. Keep in mind that the developers of this test love all things being aligned, that is, matching up, going together; so always make sure you model each of the good things that you are saying. Once your organizational health has been diagnosed, if it is found lacking in any area, you must jump on it like a firefighter on a fire. Together with your campus community members, create a plan to address and improve it. Then implement the plan and, given time, evaluate it for improvement. Above all, remember to look for and respect the common ground amongst differences of opinions and all forms of diversity as shown in Figure 2.7.

The things we do every day should be aligned with at least one goal, and every goal should lead directly to, or be *aligned* with, the vision. This is shown in Figure 2.8. If we are daily doing things that are not aligned with the campus vision, something is wrong and needs to be corrected. I do not know how to make this clearer. Everything we do should be aligned with a goal that will lead us toward our campus vision. Period. Anything else is a waste of time.

Figure 2.7   Identifying and Respecting the Common Ground

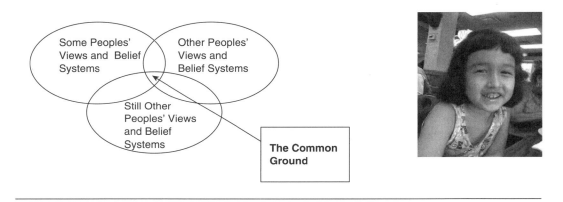

Figure 2.8   Campus Activities Should be Clearly Articulated to the District Vision

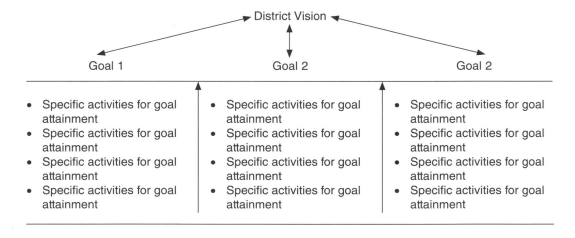

GOAL SETTING IN MORE DETAIL ◼

Just as the campus goals should be aligned with the campus vision, in an ideal situation, the campus vision should be aligned with the district vision. This generally is not a problem because there is always at least one goal that has to do with targeted academics.

Take heed. For a campus to maximize its' effectiveness, *everything* must be perfectly aligned. This includes curriculum, instruction, staff development, assessment of every kind, and the budget. All of it should be based on the needs of the students, which are aligned directly to the vision. There is no way I can stress enough how important the vision is!

So what does it mean for *everything* to be perfectly aligned? Well, let's talk about what everything includes. It includes

- campus and individual student needs;
- goals and strategies to address them;
- curriculum, which is *what* we teach;
- instruction, which is *how* we teach it (differentiated, please);
- assessment of both how students are learning (think various forms of testing) and how we are teaching;
- appropriate staff development to appropriately address the needs of the students; and
- a budget that addresses all of the above to maximize the effectiveness of our campus.

If all of these things are aligned, that is, tied to each other and working together, we will enhance the opportunities for all students, regardless of their circumstances, to learn to the best of their ability.

Again, daily school activities should be aligned with at least one goal, and all goals should be aligned with the vision. Say you have a goal that happens to be increasing campus attendance by $X\%$ in the fall semester. First, let's look at the components of that goal:

- Increasing attendance is the focus.
- By $X\%$ makes it a measureable goal. We either reach $X\%$, or we don't. We can measure that.
- "In the fall semester" is the deadline.

Remember, goals without deadlines are only dreams. We are not dreaming. We are taking action. When are we taking action? This fall. We either make our specific, measureable goal, or we don't. If we don't, we modify and adjust, but we do not give up on improving attendance!

Next, look at the specific activities we will do on a regular basis to ensure we meet each goal. Using the same attendance example, see how it aligns with the district and campus vision.

For each goal, list the specific actions the campus is going to do to reach this goal. What does this mean? It means what are the specific activities we as a campus community are going to do to ensure we have an improvement in attendance of at least $X\%$ this fall semester. Now more than one campus could have this or a similar goal, yet its activities for attainment could vary. That's fine. The activities are the things that your campus community members have defined together that they will do to ensure this goal is met. The same is true for however many goals your campus community members have chosen to undertake at this time. There is no magic number. However, collaboration and communication on the strategies for their attainment are the keys.

You must define specific activities that are going to get you from the reality of today to the vision of tomorrow. In our example, these would be specific examples of things your campus members are going to do to improve attendance by $X\%$ this fall semester.

Then make sure they get done, assessed, and modified, if necessary.

Remember the integration of technology in all of the above. Integrating technology is no longer a luxury. It is essential in differentiating instruction across the curriculum. Therefore, all forms of technology, telecommunications, and information systems should be embedded in the curriculum and instruction, and, thus in the vision–goals–strategies alignment. Consider all of this a flowchart that takes us from the student to the campus goals and, ultimately, to the vision. This is shown in Figure 2.9.

Now let's add another piece to the pie. That piece of the pie is staff development. Staff development is not just something to mark off a checklist each year. Again, it should be *aligned* with teacher needs. How do we know the teachers' needs? We look at the students' needs. How do we know the students' needs?

We look at student data.

■ DATA ANALYSIS ▶ STAFF DEVELOPMENT

Everything comes back to the students and their needs, thus, we must be constantly looking at all forms of data. This goes beyond the STARR test or any other form of testing. Yes, that is a big part of it, but it is not the only part. We should look at student daily work, their environment, their

Figure 2.9   Integrated Technology and Vision Alignment

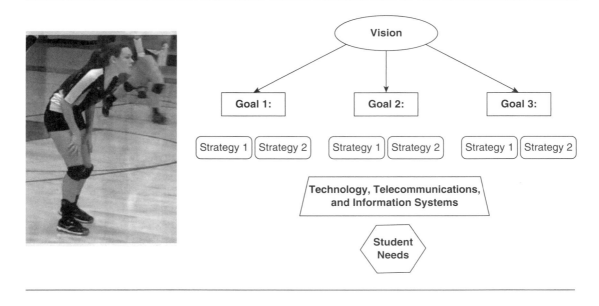

mobility, their cultural, their socio-economic levels and needs, and all other factors. We should be observing students in class. Think of everything involving each student as some form of data. Look at and analyze everything as a whole before making decisions regarding any student.

Once you know the needs of the students, by default you know the needs of the teachers. *The teachers need professional development in the areas in which their students perform the lowest.* Why? Because if these teachers could teach these concepts any better, they would be doing it. Let's take a medical example. Say someone is sick, goes to the doctor, and has blood work done. The doctor is going to focus on the areas that the blood work *shows need*, not the areas where the patient appears healthy.

Folks, we need to look at the needs, not where we are healthy. We must have a data–based needs assessment as shown in Figure 2.10 to show us where our staff development needs are. If a combination of our data, including test scores, show our students' strongest needs are in estimation and reading comprehension, then guess what our areas of targeted upcoming staff development should be? *Estimation and reading comprehension across the curriculum!*

Therefore, we move from the identified needs of the student to knowing where we should conduct meaningful staff development. The staff development should include components where the teachers are trained in individualized/differentiated/culturally sensitive instruction with actual examples of how they can do these methods in their classrooms across the curriculum. Together, all of this will maximize our efforts toward goal and vision attainment.

Figure 2.10   Use Data From Multiple Sources in Decision Making

---

DATA–BASED NEEDS ASSESSMENT	
Source 1:	**Source 2:**
Source 3:	**Source 4:**
Staff Development Needed	Staff Development Needed

■ DATA ANALYSIS ▶BUDGET DEVELOPMENT

The same model is used to determine how to build a budget. There are certain things that are always necessary in any campus or district budget. However, there is also some leeway, particularly in the area of curricular materials. How do we know what should be budgeted for?

Together with the teachers, we look at the same data that determined our staff development and identified the greatest needs of our students. From there we build the budget built on these same needs of the students. The teachers should be the ones to prioritize the items they determine most necessary in meeting those needs. Other stakeholders such as the site-based team are also involved. But the most important thing to remember about building a budget is that it is always built around the needs of the students. Therefore, the budget and the vision must support each other. The second most important thing to remember about a budget is that once you have it, you stay in it. You don't want the central office to be replacing you with someone who can add and subtract!

As a part of the budget being created, teachers determine and prioritize the resources they will need to accomplish the specified goals to meet students' needs. Please notice how *everything* comes back to the students' needs. But buying things alone does not meet the students' needs nor does it solve problems. You must lead the teachers to develop and implement effective teaching strategies to best use the resources to actually improve learning. *Teaching is not about test scores*. It is about improving learning.

The improved-teaching produced and procured strategies should lead to the campus goals that must be aligned with the vision. Thus, everything fits together like a fine-fitting puzzle where lots of pieces come together to create magnificent student success.

■ OBSTACLES TO SUCCESS

Whereas everything we have discussed may sound easy or hard, depending on your perspective and your own personal leadership philosophy, in truth, regardless, you will face obstacles. For example, no matter who is president of the United States or which party is in office, the president is always faced with obstacles. Accept the fact that obstacles exist, and life isn't always easy. The real question is how can we turn obstacles into student–focused learning opportunities? This is the question we must *continuously* be asking ourselves as well as asking our teachers also to reflect upon. Until we can answer that question, each time an obstacle arises, we will not have genuine school reform. We will not create ideal schools, and we will not be ideal principals.

I know I am a Pollyanna. You may have decided you have never heard from such a Pollyanna toward school leadership in your entire life. But at least I am a sincere Pollyanna. I mean every word I have said. What's more, I invite you to believe it with me. Together we can make a difference. Together we are not alone. As Margaret Mead said, and I paraphrase, it just takes one person to start a change movement.

Will you come along with me?

DOMAIN I   ■

Now we will go into detail regarding Domain I, School Community Leadership. The three main concepts for you to remember in Domain I are the school vision, which we have discussed, the school climate, and the school culture.

What is the school community? The competencies define it as including students, staff, parents/caregivers, and community members.

For our purposes we can say the school community involves *everyone* or *all* people. Always look for answers that address the needs of everyone or all students, not just some of the students. They will throw in responses that sound good but do not address the needs of all students. Therefore, those are not good answers—even if they sound good.

> **Competency 001:** *The principal knows how to shape campus culture by facilitating the development, articulation, implementation, and stewardship of a vision of learning that is shared and supported by the school community.*

There is a huge amount of information in there. I often tell students, if they can nail this competency and can apply the same concepts throughout the test, they will pass the test.

Positive Versus Negative Verbs

First, let's look at the initial verb. It is *shape*. *Shape* is a *positive* verb. It implies the principal worked with the school community to develop the vision. The principal *collaborated* with the school community. Because everyone worked together to *develop* or *create* the vision, they will support it. Why? People support what they help create.

Always look for positive verbs in answer choices. If a verb is negative, it is a wrong answer. This is shown in Figure 2.11.

How can you tell if a verb is positive or negative? Let's look at these examples:

1. Justify vs. clarify

2. Encourage vs. scold

3. Mentor vs. discipline

Make note! If an answer has a negative verb in it at all, it is a wrong answer. Remember how much time we focused on the ideal principal last time? Well, here it is in action. The ideal principal is never negative. The ideal principal is always positive.

Therefore, as we go through all the competencies, you will notice that they always use positive verbs like the principal "shapes" the campus culture rather than the principal "tells" the campus what the culture will be. Autocratic or top-down principal actions are never correct.

Figure 2.11   Watch Your Verbs!

- Positive Verbs = Right Answers
- Negative Verbs = Wrong Answers
- The Ideal Principal never does anything negative!

The nine competencies define the ideal principal. The ideal principal may not/will not be realistic. Why? The test developers know you know what reality looks like. You live in it every day. They want to know if you know what ideal looks like.

The next important word is *facilitating*, which comes from the root word *facilitate*. To facilitate something means that you are not necessarily doing everything, but you are seeing to it, or facilitating, that everything does, indeed, get done. *Facilitate* is one of the test developers' favorite verbs, so watch for it. When you see the word *facilitate*, or any of its derivatives, in an answer, PAY ATTENTION! If they do not use the word, but they use the meaning, it is just as good. Mark it. It is one of their favorites.

Remember the Elaine Wilmore 1–2–3–4 Plan. Review Figure 2.4. If you can count to four, you can get every question on the test that asks you the "initial" or "first" thing the principal would do. You start by looking at the answers for a #1. If you find it, mark it. NOTHING COMES BEFORE #1. We are not dealing in negative numbers here!

If you do not see a #1, look for a #2, and so on. The thing to remember is to never skip numbers, that is, never skip steps!

So what exactly is the 1–2–3–4 that I am so big on?

1. Develop, create, or plan whatever you are doing.

2. Articulate, or communicate and explain, or clarify what is to be done.

3. Implement, or actually put your plan into action.

4. Steward is to be a good caretaker of people and all resources of the resources, including programs that we have. In the rest of the

competencies the concept of evaluation or assessment or measurement is often used. Remember, what gets measured gets done, so all goals should be measureable.

After the 1–2–3–4 Plan, the competency puts the focus on the vision of learning, which we discussed extensively, that is shared and supported by the school community. These are also concepts we have discussed. Communicate and collaborate with all stakeholders—which means virtually everyone.

After the competency itself comes the "bullets" or "A, B, Cs" of examples of things the principal does that are a part of Competency 001. It will be that way through all nine competencies. My *Passing the Principal TExES Exam (2nd ed.)* goes into detail regarding not just every competency but every subcompetency. That is not the purpose of this book. Read that book, and make it your own. Make sure you thoroughly understand each competency before moving forward with this book.

> **Competency 002:** *The principal knows how to communicate and collaborate with all members of the school community, respond to diverse interests and needs, and mobilize resources to promote student success.*

Competency 002 moves the focus to communication and collaboration. In short, everything is about student success. If we are doing anything at school that is not about student success, why? In order to do this we must be good communicators. We must be able to ensure others understand what we are trying to say—and I do not mean this exclusive to language barriers. There are people that speak English all day long, but they have difficulty with people understanding them. I had a statistics professor when I was working on my doctorate. He spoke English. We still didn't understand a word he said. Thank goodness for a good text because he simply was not a good teacher. Good teachers and leaders must be good communicators.

Collaboration is a big deal on this test and for success as a principal. It means you do not make decisions in your office with the door closed. It means you involve as many people as possible in decision making. Site-based management, at its purest, was designed to be a perfect model of collaboration. Sometimes it is. Sometimes it isn't. But, the fact remains, get the opinions of others. Involve all people. Make decisions together. Collaborate!

Next, we respond, not ignore, to diverse, or different, interests and needs of our stakeholders. The two keys are *respond* and *diverse*. We must be paying attention, constantly looking for improvement, and making data-driven decisions in order to even know the interests and needs of our students. Also, *diverse* means different. This is not exclusive to race. It includes gender, learning styles, faiths—everything. We must be responsive to everything that makes our students unique individuals; no two are ever exactly alike.

Last, in Competency 002, we mobilize resources to promote student success. I love the verb *mobilize*. It is such a strong positive verb. It always makes me think the Marines are coming! What it really means is, if we do not have the resources to do something that needs to be done to promote student success, we find them elsewhere. We "mobilize" by working together with the district and the school community to come up with everything that is needed to promote student success. You are thinking, "That's not reasonable!"

So what? It's ideal.

> **Competency 003:** *The principal knows how to act with integrity, fairness, and in an ethical and legal manner.*

This is the *ethics* competency. We wish we didn't need it, but we do. We wish everyone would act right all of the time, but they don't. We wish every educator was an advocate for all children, but not all are.
Are you?
Remember when we were little and were invited to a birthday party, how our mothers would always say, "Be nice. Say thank you. Mind your manners"?
Being a principal is like being at a big party. Always be nice, say thank you, and mind your manners. But it is more than that. Be aware of and follow the *Code of Ethics and Standard Practices for Texas Educators*. Be an advocate for every child. Speak up for those who can't speak up for themselves. As shown in Figure 2.12, treat all students with respect regardless of how old they are. That's what being a true educational leader is all about.

■ DOMAIN II

Now we are going to look at Domain II, Instructional Leadership. Domain II is the largest domain within the test framework, which means it has the

Figure 2.12   Respect

- Always treat everyone with respect regardless of age or other factors.

most questions on the test. It is also where you should excel because, after all, you are already a wonderful teacher that individualizes for every student, right?

> **Competency 004:** *The principal knows how to facilitate the design and implementation of curricula and strategic plans that enhance teaching and learning; ensure alignment of curriculum, instruction, resources, and assessment; and promote the use of varied assessments to measure student performance.*

There is a lot said in this, so we are going to take it piece by piece and break it down into small pieces of a very large pie.

Remember that *facilitate* is one of the test developers' very favorite verbs, so when you see *facilitate* in a test answer, look at it very carefully. *With "facilitate," they are acknowledging that you are not responsible for doing and knowing everything, but you ARE responsible for seeing to it that everything gets done.*

Therefore, as principal you are responsible for facilitating (not doing it yourself) the design (#1 from the 1–2–3–4 Plan), implementation (#3 from the 1–2–3–4 Plan) of curricula (what we teach), and strategic plans (long-term lesson planning, vertical and horizontal alignment, etc.) that enhance (make something better) teaching (what we do) and learning (what the students do). There is a lot in there so read it again, over and over, very carefully to make sure you understand it. It is also spelled out word for word in *Passing the Principal TExES Exam: Keys to Certification and School Leadership (2nd ed.).*

Next, it says to *ensure* (guarantee; we are serious about this!) alignment (making sure everything goes together and matches; e.g., the Texas Essential Knowledge and Skills [TEKS] with what we are actually teaching) of curriculum (what we teach) and instruction (how we teach it). The goal is to individualize or differentiate to meet the individual needs of every student.

Resources are the things we need to teach and do our jobs, whereas assessment is measuring what we are teaching and how students are learning. Remember, if our students are not doing well on our assessments, it means we are not doing well on how we are teaching. Think about that for a while. It is never the child's fault for not learning. It is our fault for not differentiating to meet his or her needs.

The last piece of the competency says we promote (encourage) the use of varied (diverse or different kinds of) assessments to measure student performance. This is shown in Figure 2.13. For example, Johnny may not be able to pass a test on engines. But if you ask him to take one apart, fix it, and put it back together, he can easily do it. So, does Johnny know anything about engines or not?

So, in summary, Competency 004 is about aligning and individualizing everything we do to enhance and ensure student learning. Competency 004 takes teaching and learning as serious business, not status quo. So should we.

Figure 2.13   Alternative Forms of Assessment

- Create alternative forms of assessment.

Competency 005: *The principal knows how to advocate, nurture, and sustain an instructional program and a campus culture that are conducive to student learning and staff professional growth.*

Competency 005, in some ways, reminds me of the "stewardship" in Competency 001 because it says the principal knows how to *advocate, nurture, and sustain*—stop right there. Can you think of a better definition of *stewardship* than to advocate, nurture, and sustain something?

So Competency 005 is all about being a good steward of an instructional program (see Competency 004) and a campus culture (see Competency 001) that are conducive to student learning and staff professional growth.

See, you just thought you were going to get off easy on Competency 005 with references to prior competencies. Then it hits you with staff professional growth.

Staff professional growth includes *all* of us, even you and me. We should constantly be seeking to be lifelong learners. On the test, questions will be designed to determine if you know that professional development is aligned with the needs of the students as determined by looking at the data (data-based decision making). This is shown in Figure 2.14.

As previously shown in Figure 2.10, the data include test scores and other materials. The test will also be looking to see that you know that staff development (which is the same thing as professional development) is designed to create lifelong learners out of all of us.

So, while you may think that you are finished learning when you graduate and pass this test, you are allowed to relax and celebrate for at least 15 minutes. After that, continue reading, researching, and learning. Model being a lifelong learner for your staff. Let your walk match your talk. Never just tell them to do something without modeling it yourself. March on, learners!

Figure 2.14   Professional Development

- Is for everyone.
- Should meet the needs of students by meeting the needs of staff.

Competency 006: *The principal knows how to implement a staff evaluation and development system to improve the performance of all staff members, select and implement appropriate models for supervision and staff development, and apply the legal requirements for personnel management.*

Notice that when it says a "staff evaluation and development system," it does not say the Professional Development and Assessment System (PDAS) because PDAS is not required by law in Texas. What is required is either PDAS or another instrument that measures the same things. Therefore, you will not see the term PDAS on the test. Even that is changing, but it is not on the test yet.

You are also not required to have had Instructional Leadership Development (ILD) or PDAS training before you take the test. If you have had it, bravo! You have been exposed to more knowledge, which will make you more knowledgeable for the test. But you are not required to have had either, nor will there be any questions that require you to have been through ILD or PDAS.

So, what is the purpose of a "staff evaluation and *development* system?" The goal is to help everyone improve, even your good teachers. ALL of us have room to grow. We should never be satisfied with the status quo. We should always be seeking to improve because when we improve, the greater the chances of our students' learning improving also!

"Select and implement appropriate models for supervision and staff development," which means use appropriate walk-throughs, and so on, for all staff, not just some of the staff and "apply the legal requirements for personnel management." Keep everything legal, obviously.

No matter what happens, every teacher gets due process. Secondly, in the end, only the board hires and only the board fires. You can *recommend.*

But the board makes the final decision every time, and that is AFTER due process has occurred.

> **Competency 007:** *The principal knows how to apply organizational, decision-making, and problem-solving skills to ensure an effective learning environment.*

While it may seem short, *do not overlook it*! This one is all about how you think, make decisions, use data, and solve problems. In essence, it is about your core values because they will show when you have to make difficult decisions particularly involving data.

You think I am exaggerating, but I am not. Sometimes you will have to solve a problem or make a decision that is not going to be popular with the teachers, but it is the right thing to do for the students. Therefore, it is what you have to do. Be strong!

Don't let the bureaucrats or the everyday whiners get to you! Be strong! Always, always, always think of what is RIGHT for the students, NOT what is easy or popular.

Let me paraphrase a story, *The Animal School,* by George H. Reavis. It is about a monkey, a fish, a duck, a lion, and some other animals. All of them had to take a test. There was only one question on the test: "How do you climb a tree?"

The monkey, having been raised in a treed environment, knew the answer and scored well on the test.

But, neither the fish, the duck, the lion, nor the other animals had any idea how to climb a tree because their cultural environment had absolutely nothing to do with climbing trees. Their teacher did not differentiate instruction or assessment for them; so what do you think happened?

They flunked the test.

You say, "Elaine, that's a funny story."

Well, it would be if it wasn't so true and so sad. We teach monkeys, fish, ducks, and lions every day, but do we make our teaching relevant for all of them?

And with that, I leave you to think about it. Teach everyone: monkeys, fish, ducks, and lions alike. Teach them as if your life depended upon it!

■ DOMAIN III

Now we address our last domain, Domain III, Administrative Leadership. It is the shortest of the three domains and only has two competencies in it.

Whereas Domains I and II were about *leading* the school, Domain III is still about leading, but it is also about *managing* the school.

Prior to now, we have not discussed basic things like the commodes going out in the little boys' restrooms (or worse, in the teachers' restrooms!), the roof blowing off the school, any type of crisis management that is becoming more and more prevalent in society today—or just the everyday things you do as CEO managing the campus.

These everyday things, or actually running the school, constitute Domain III. The three main themes of Domain III are finance, facilities, and student safety.

> **Competency 008:** *The principal knows how to apply principles of effective leadership and management in relation to campus budgeting, personnel, resource utilization, financial management, and technology use.*

As with all the other competencies, it is important to note this one starts with "The principal knows how to . . ." do something. In Competency 008 and Competency 009 each say "to apply principles of effective leadership *and management* . . ."

Notice these are the only two times we see that phrase or the word *management* included. As David Erlandson of Texas A&M once said, "It is hard to keep your eyes on the vision of the school (Domain I) when the walls are falling down around you."

Naturally, we don't want any walls falling down anywhere, thus we have Domain III.

As shown in Figure 2.15, laws and policies are the basic operational structures of all schools and districts.

Figure 2.15   Law and Policy Provide a School's Basic Operating Structure

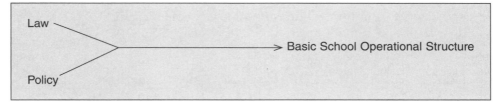

In Competency 008 we focus on these in five ways.

1. *Campus Budgeting*: There are two very important things to remember about the campus budget.

    a. *Stay in it*. If you are repeatedly overdrawn on an account, the superintendent may decide to replace you with someone that can add and subtract.

    b. Build it collaboratively *BASED ON THE NEEDS OF THE STUDENTS.*

Whether you are building the budget or developing curriculum or professional development, it must ALWAYS be based on the NEEDS OF THE STUDENTS and nothing else. Period. This flowchart is shown in Figure 2.16.

Remember, *everything* we do in school, every single little thing, **must** be based on the *needs of the students* as determined by data analysis and watching the ways each student learns. If we do not do this, we are wasting valuable time. The budget must support the vision. The vision must support the budget. It is a cyclical process as shown in Figure 2.17.

2. *Personnel*: We covered professional development in Domain II. Here we are basically referring to hiring and firing. In relation to both, an important thing to remember is that although it may commonly be said, "I hired so and so . . ." the truth is, you only *recommended* the hiring of anyone. In the end, only the board can hire, and only the board can fire. Sometimes hiring can be unofficially delegated to the superintendent in large districts for high-need areas (math, science, ESL, SPED, etc.), but the truth is nothing is official until the board takes action.

Figure 2.16   Budget Vision Alignment

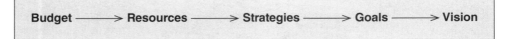

Figure 2.17   The Budget and the Vision Must Support Each Other

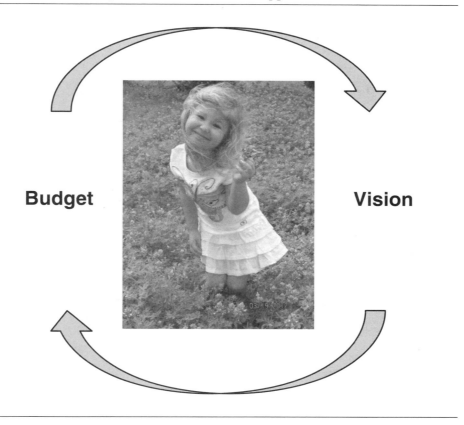

Budget   Vision

The same is true for firing. No matter how ridiculous someone may have acted, they still get *due process*. Remember that for questions on the test and for life! Then, again, only the board can actually separate someone from the district. It is even the board who accepts resignations.

3. *Resource Utilization*: Remember the word *steward* way back in Competency 001? Think of it again here in reference to resource utilization. Tax dollars are not growing on trees. Few districts have as much money as they need or wish they had. Therefore, it is prudent for all educators, particularly principals, to be good stewards of the resources, or things, we have. Don't waste things. Use things sparingly. Treat your school budget as you would your home budget and use it carefully. Remember, if you spend everything in the fall, it is going to be a very long spring semester.

4. *Fiscal Management*: Fiscal management is tied directly to resource utilization. Plan ahead for what your needs will be and when they will occur. Save budgeted funds for projects that occur once a year. Don't hoard money, but do not spend it excessively either. Again, exercise good fiscal management at school just as you would at home.

5. *Technology Use*: Any school that is not appropriately using technology is living in the wrong century. Have a campus technology committee to help plan for the needs and utilization of the campus in relation to technology. *Remember licensing laws*. An appropriate use of technology is not more "drill and kill" work-type sheets that just happen to be done on a

computer. Last, and I hate to say this, but it must be said! No porn on school computers! That is a very good way to get yourself or someone on your staff fired.

Competency 009: *The principal knows how to apply principles of effective leadership and management to the campus physical plant and support systems to ensure a safe and effective learning environment.*

You will notice that the first 11 words of Competency 009 are identical to Competency 008. Then they differ. The issue is to apply principles of leadership and management to the *campus physical plant and support systems.*

What are the "campus physical plant and support systems?" The campus physical plant is the total buildings and land that the school is sitting on. If there is a football stadium or a baseball field on your campus, they are a part of your physical plant. A band hall? Physical plant. What about a cafeteria? An agriculture arena? An industrial arts area/whatever? All of those are a part of the campus physical plant. So the physical plant is more than just the classrooms. It is *all* of the campus that supports and serves the students.

That means if the roof blows off, while it may not be your job to get up there and fix it, it is your job to *facilitate* that it gets done. You follow district policy, whatever the policy may be. The same holds true for any other problem that relates to the buildings, and so on. Follow district policy, and you can never go wrong.

The last portion is the *why* of the *issue*. Why do we need an efficient and effectively running physical plant? *To ensure a safe and effective learning environment.* Sound familiar?

What does a safe and effective learning environment mean? It means we have a campus *climate* that is *conducive to teachers teaching and students learning.* Period. If the climate in a school is not supportive and nurturing, learning will not be maximized. I hope you take that last sentence serious because it can make or break you.

And that, folks, pretty much sums up Domain III.

That's the big overview of what the domains and competencies include. Now let us move on to the case study chapters where we will have actual case studies that are aligned with each of the competencies themselves. They will make the words of the competencies become real to you in daily scenarios. Enjoy and learn!

SECTION II

DOMAIN I: SCHOOL COMMUNITY LEADERSHIP

3

Competency 001

It's All About the Vision

Key Concepts: School Culture, School Climate, School Vision

Competency 001: *The principal knows how to shape campus culture by facilitating the development, articulation, implementation, and stewardship of a vision of learning that is shared and supported by the school community.*

■ CASE STUDY 1: RETAINING POTENTIAL DROPOUTS

Principal Fernando Alaniz and his staff are greatly concerned about the dropout rate of Hispanic students beginning at the eighth grade and how this pass-through impacts their high school. They are dedicated to a stewardship of a vision of learning that includes all students. As they begin an intense study as to causes and prevention efforts to keep students in school, they realize this study includes massive amounts of time spent in home visits conducted in Spanish and English with both students and parents, oral surveys, and the disaggregation of these data. Since there are only so many hours in the day, this project protrudes significantly into their after-school time. Their goal is to determine the causes of the high dropout rate that begins before students ever arrive at their high school and to initiate steps to prevent it from either continuing or escalating.

Individual and Group Reflective Questions:

1. Assemble a plan to achieve the desired Hispanic dropout reduction rate. The plan must be effective but less cumbersome and time consuming than what they are currently doing.

2. Compile and categorize factors causing students to drop out in the first place. Brainstorm ways to prevent these from happening.

3. Develop a reasonable plan where staff putting in unreasonable amounts of time on the project could receive comp time for their efforts.

4. Establish benchmarks for formal and informal assessment of the project.

5. Formulate a plan to measure the project's success or failure.

This flowchart is previously shown in Figure 2.16.

Figure 3.1   Competency-Based Principals Are Visionaries

- Develop a Campus Vision
- Articulate the Campus Vision
- Implement the Campus Vision
- Are Good Stewards of the Campus Vision

CASE STUDY 2:   ■
STUDENT LEADERSHIP ACADEMY

Prairie Grove ISD has gone to an almost total freedom-of-choice campus selection system for K–12. Each school is built around a theme. Throughout the district, multiple open houses are held each spring so families can know what their options and themes are. George W. Bush Leadership Academy has chosen to base its curriculum around a student-leadership emphasis where students are highly involved in the leadership aspects of every facet of the school from curriculum, as possible, to cocurricular. Students wear uniforms and come from all portions of the ISD. They are working very hard to develop, articulate, implement, and be a steward of a vision of learning for all students who may choose to attend George W. Bush Leadership Academy. Although there are adults present for each student-led club and committee, the students do take the lead in most areas. This involves an enormous amount of ahead-of-time work as teachers and the principal work with student leaders to equip them with the knowledge they need to know. As a result of the buy-in from the school community as well as the structure of the school, student test scores are high.

Individual and Group Reflective Questions:

1. What are the pros and cons of a student led leadership academy, particularly on the elementary level?

2. Are students, particularly elementary students, mature enough to take on these leadership roles?

3. What are the pros and cons of a district balancing multiple types of schools/academies across their school districts at the same time?

4. Why would student scores potentially be higher in a public academy of choice rather than a traditional school?

5. Would academic-themed academies work well in your district? Why, or why not?

■ CASE STUDY 3: VISION MISALIGNMENT

The demographics of the neighborhood as well as Benjamin Franklin Intermediate School have changed significantly in the past five years. Fewer students come from dual parent homes. More live in rental properties resulting in a higher mobility rate, and fewer have a first language of English.

The teachers at Benjamin Franklin are torn regarding their mission statement. Some teachers strongly feel it should be changed to align with the changing demographics of the school community. Other teachers feel equally strongly that it should remain the same, and that all students should rise to the same standard. Principal Barnard Kastler understands the importance of a vision and goals that are shared and supported by the school community. Thus far, no community input has been procured because some of the teachers do not feel any change is necessary, thus, meeting with parents is a waste of time. Mr. Kastler is challenged to bring together the opposing views into one cohesive mission statement with appropriately aligned goals.

Individual and Group Reflective Questions:

1. Why is a mission statement important to a school?

2. How can changing demographics impact the mission of a campus?

3. Describe a change model Mr. Kastler could implement to resolve the conflict above.

4. Explain reasons why, or why not, parental involvement is necessary in making important school decisions.

5. Can all students be held to the same standards?

PRACTICE COMPETENCY QUESTIONS ■

1. Mr. Hawthorne was recently hired as the new principal of Hope Intermediate School. The school has been hindered by a dilemma because the past administrators, teachers, and support staff have an apathetic morale and have accepted low performance as the norm. Mr. Hawthorne is faced with the challenge of addressing this attitude of neglect. Expectations and standards need to be readdressed to ensure the success of all students regardless of the students' backgrounds. In this situation, Mr. Hawthorne should consider which of the following when addressing the needs of the campus?

   A. Meet individually with teachers and staff, and remind them of the importance of participating in the efforts to improve school performance

   B. Analyze the student performance data with teachers, and help them identify instructional areas that should be addressed and modified

   C. Ask teachers to meet with their teams, and develop new campus goals for instructional improvement

   D. Explain that he is not happy with the school's past performance, and implement a new plan without the involvement or support of the staff

The correct answer is B.

2. Mr. Vosburg is the principal at North High School. Behavior issues and students receiving District Alternative Educational Placement (DAEP) disciplinary action have been on a significant rise in the past year and have had a significantly negative impact on the campus culture and climate. Mr. Vosburg formed a committee to discuss a new program called Positive Behavior Intervention (PBI), which will need support from faculty. The committee has agreed upon program goals and objectives and to move forward with implementation of the plan. How can Mr. Vosburg best facilitate and assure the longevity of the PBI?

   A. Define the program and upcoming changes in a faculty meeting

   B. Administer literature about the program to all faculty

   C. Ensure time for staff training and meeting availability to address questions

   D. Introduce the program to department leads, and have them implement the program as a trial

The correct answer is C.

3. To further enhance the adjustment of programs and processes to improve student learning, Mr. Vosberg should

   A. create a committee that includes one teacher from each campus to review the survey results.

   B. do a complete reorganization of the staff members.

    C. work closely with the Parent-Teacher Organization (PTO) to relay information

    D. survey parents and other stakeholders about their perceptions and suggestions for improvement toward the campus vision.

The correct answer is D.

4. After completion of the surveys, Mr. Vosberg creates a committee to review them. In addition to campus administration, who should be a part of this committee?

    I. All teachers

    II. One member from each grade level or department

    III. All parents

    IV. Several parents from each grade level

    A. I only

    B. I and IV

    C. III only

    D. II and IV

The correct answer is D.

5. The teachers at Manchester High School participate on the committee to develop the campus vision and goals and generally enjoy working with their principal, Ms. Davis. During a recent planning meeting to review campus data, the teachers expressed their frustration for not having adequate time to meet and collaborate with their team. They feel that if they had more time during the day to plan together and design interventions there would be an improvement in overall student achievement. After careful consideration and research, Mrs. Davis makes changes to the master schedule. Teachers will now have their conference periods with other teachers of the same subject and grade. This will allow them to have more time to collaborate. The changes to the schedule show that she

    I. listens to her staff.

    II. implements strategies that ensure effective collaboration.

    III. establishes procedures to assess and modify implementation plans to ensure the achievement of the campus vision.

    IV. is concerned about the safety of the campus.

    A. I and III

    B. I and II

    C. I, II, and III

    D. I and IV

The correct answer is C.

4

Competency 002

Do You Hear What I Am Really Saying?

Key Concepts: School Culture, School Climate, School Vision

Competency 002: *The principal knows how to communicate and collaborate with all members of the school community, respond to diverse interests and needs, and mobilize resources to promote student success.*

CASE STUDY 1: HAPPY TALK ■

Rolling Pastures is a residential and day charter school with students from around the world, particularly Asia. There is an emphasis on college prep and on working with animals of various kinds and being in the outdoors. The school is K–12 with approximately 400 day and residential students. All students participate in agricultural events to varying extents. The arts and other cocurricular activities are also emphasized, but agricultural issues and being in wide open spaces carries the biggest emphasis.

Because of the wide diversity of cocurricular activities, Principal Petra Greggory is interested in improving the communication and collaboration of all members of the school community and responding to their diverse interests and needs. To that end, the idea of a digital campus newsletter was developed that not only could be shared with the residential and day students but also with their families around the world. Although at first it was thought the newsletter could be added as a part of the school's Web site, it quickly outgrew that capacity. This resulted in multiple technological issues, but the campus was determined to carry on the idea because of their commitment to communicating and collaborating with all internal and external members of the school community. This showed Rolling Pastures's commitment to facilitating the use of technology, telecommunications, and information systems to enrich the campus curriculum and cocurricular activities.

Individual and Group Reflective Questions:

1. What would have been the difference between a regular paper newsletter and all the drama of creating an online campus newspaper?

2. Outline the steps in developing a major campus project such as an online newsletter.

3. How could you, as principal, assess the success of an online newsletter?

4. Would input from the parents from around the world be necessary in an online campus newsletter?

5. If so, how could this be done?

Figure 4.1   Competency-Based Principals Are Collaborative

- Collaborating with Families and Other Community Members
- Responding to Community Interests and Needs
- Mobilizing Community Resources

■ CASE STUDY 2: BAD COMMUNICATION

A teacher, Ms. Gideon, is told by Mrs. Frozen, the principal, she will receive a reimbursement for approved mileage to and from a conference. Ms. Gideon must enter specific data inside a software program. The problem is she has never been trained in the program, and no one is around or willing to show her how to do it. This leaves Ms. Gideon feeling frustrated that no one cared if she was able to enter the data or if conditions were created to encourage achievement of the campus vision. The more she tries, and the more frustrated she gets, the less she finds the campus facilitating the use and integration of technology for faculty, much less for students.

In her attempts to navigate the program, she gets locked out of the computer system. The program says her password is wrong, but it had just been updated within the last 10 days. Ms. Gideon called the IT department and was told that the program had its own password that she would need to get from Human Resources (HR).

She calls HR and is told to call Jim Henderson in Accounts Payable. Already frustrated when she calls Jim, she receives a message that his mailbox is full, thank you, and good-bye.

By now Ms. Gideon is incredibly exasperated over the lack of communication and help. She goes back to her campus office, explains her frustration, and is told that maybe Miss Marie can help. Miss Marie is able to provide enough direction for Ms. Gideon to figure the rest of the program out for herself. The reimbursement is finally entered into the system, and she is eventually reimbursed. Nevertheless, Ms. Gideon is left with a feeling that the culture and climate of the school does not care if she is ever reimbursed, and that the internal communication strategies for helping her be successful are sorely lacking.

Individual and Group Reflective Questions:

1. Obviously, there was a lack of communication regarding both the software utilization and reimbursement procurement. Define a communication plan for each that would facilitate the process.

2. Should Ms. Gideon have had so many problems with the software and no one being available to help her when she had been on an approved trip? How could the problem have been remedied?

Figure 4.2   Families Are Important in the Education of Their Children

3. The lack of communication between the various departments is an entirely different story. Outline a procedure that would facilitate making the procurement of appropriate information a smooth process.

4. What was Mrs. Frozen's role in this scenario? What should she have done to help the situation?

5. Develop a checklist of steps to do to be reimbursed for approved travel.

CASE STUDY 3: VERTICAL ■ AND HORIZONTAL *WHAT?*

Mr. Jolly, the principal of Misty Meadows Elementary, is frustrated and more than a little bit embarrassed. The district is making a big push this year on both vertical and horizontal alignment of curriculum. Although

Mr. Jolly has attended all of the in-service trainings that the district has provided, he is still confused and uncertain how to lead his campus in this endeavor. He understands that the teachers and staff will be looking to him for leadership on how to vertically and horizontally align the curriculum, but, frankly, he does not feel competent to do this. He is also embarrassed because he feels he should know how to do this—but doesn't. He understands that the entire campus, starting with him, needs to promote the continuous and appropriate development of all students via vertical and horizontal alignment, and he must lead in promoting an awareness of learning differences, multicultural awareness, gender sensitivity, and ethnic appreciation in this effort. Borrowing from Domain II, he also understands both he and the staff need to engage in ongoing professional development activities to enhance their knowledge and skills as well as to model lifelong learning. He is simply unsure how to go about doing all of this.

Individual and Group Reflective Questions:

1. Compare and contrast vertical and horizontal curriculum alignment.

2. Why is curriculum alignment important? Or is it?

3. Is this an issue Mr. Jolly can simply ignore and hope no one finds out? Why, or why not?

4. What would be Mr. Jolly's best first steps since he does not understand vertical and horizontal alignment?

5. How can Mr. Jolly build in an accountability framework to ensure that both he and the campus use the vertical and horizontal alignment process?

■ PRACTICE COMPETENCY QUESTIONS

1. Which of the following examples of communication methods for sharing information with parents would be the most effective in a neighborhood with a majority of low socioeconomic households?

   A. Setting up a public blog for parents to share their ideas on the school's upcoming antibullying campaign and how the community can work together to minimize this type of activity.

   B. Creating a school Facebook page to invite parents, friends, and family to the upcoming fall festival.

   C. Printing a weekly newsletter with all the upcoming events and vital information placed in a communication folder that goes home weekly.

   D. Posting all event information for parent-teacher conferences and sign-up on the school's website.

   The correct answer is C.

2. The new elementary principal visits with several staff members and recognizes the anxiety many feel regarding several changes that have occurred including having a new principal, a new counselor, six new teachers, and a new instructional coach. What steps could the principal take to decrease staff members' anxiety and increase cohesiveness, communication, and unity?

   I. Send an e-mail presenting the new staff members and explaining that everything will be fine if everyone will work as a team and commit to the district goals

   II. Spend a day before school starts conducting a team building retreat so staff members can get to know each other in an informal setting

   III. Spend time with teachers learning the culture and collaborating to establish meaningful goals for students and staff to pursue

   IV. Communicate a vision to students, staff, and parents regarding the goals and mission of the campus

   A. II and III

   B. I and III

   C. II, III, and IV

   D. I and IV

The correct answer is C.

3. As the incoming principal in a school in disarray, you immediately notice conflict among teachers in many departments, specifically the science department. When asked what the main problem is, most teachers indicate poor communication from the department head to the rest of the department. In order to gain stability within the science department you

   I. keep the department head the same because she has done it before, even though her communication skills indicate otherwise.

   II. replace the department head with a young and energetic, yet under qualified, volunteer.

   III. ask all volunteers to fill out an application for the department head position, interview those who are both qualified and willing to serve.

   IV. establish roles, functions, accountability systems, and duties for the department head.

   A. I only

   B. I and IV only

   C. II and IV only

   D. III and IV only

The correct answer is D.

4. The literacy initiative at Mt. Vernon Middle School is very poor regardless of administration's attempts to increase reading and writing in each subject area and grade level. As principal, what should you do?

   A. Collaborate with teachers in all content and grade areas to reach a consensus regarding next steps for the initiative

   B. Issue a school mandated "literacy warm-up" in every class

   C. Tell the teachers to submit lesson plans that highlight their literacy initiatives in their classroom

   D. Place teachers who are not doing the literacy initiative in their classrooms on growth plans

The correct answer is A.

5. Melda Cole Ward Intermediate School has been trying a new approach to math instruction for the past 3 years, but the results have been disappointing. The principal is putting together a team to consider this problem and identify possible solutions. Originally, the team was going to include the principal, an assistant principal, teachers from different grade levels, and the district math coordinator. The principal then decided to include parent representatives as well. Which of the following is likely to be the most important benefit of the principal's decision?

   A. Expanding the range of perspectives and ideas that will be brought to the problem-solving process

   B. Communicating to the school community the school's strong commitment to addressing the math problem

   C. Encouraging the development of a team dynamic that is more positive, balanced, and productive

   D. Increasing recognition among various school constituencies that school staff members value their input on education issues

The correct answer is A.

5

Competency 003

Why Should We Even Need *to Be Told?*

Key Concepts: School Culture, School Climate, School Vision

Competency 003: *The principal knows how to act with integrity, fairness, and in an ethical and legal manner.*

CASE STUDY 1: MISTAKE MESSAGE ■

The principal, Ms. James, of Hanes Middle School did not have a reputation for cultivating a warm campus culture or climate. In fact, she was straight forward to the point of bordering on, and stepping over, into rude. She showed little to no concern for anyone's feelings, thus, she had earned the nickname of Ms. Brick, as in hard as a brick. She did have three teachers that she seemed to like and with them was the only time anyone, including staff, ever saw her smile.

One day she sent out an innocuous email message to the entire staff that of itself was not controversial. Yet shortly thereafter, she sent another one that simply said, "No! No! No!" with no explanation. As faculty scratched their heads as to what such a stark message could mean, she did it again. "No! No! No!"

Then the next morning, just to make sure everyone understood, she sent it a third time, "No! No! No!"

None of the messages gave any explanation as to what she was talking about or what was so important that the faculty not do. It was assumed that the three "No!" messages were in reference to the prior innocuous message, but no one understood why there was a necessity for three "No!" messages with no explanation whatsoever. The faculty was left to wonder if this was modeling and promoting the highest standard of conduct, ethical principles, and integrity in decision making, actions, and behaviors or if it was a good manifestation of the Code of Ethics and Standard Practices for Texas Educators. In fact, they were perplexed.

Figure 5.1   Competency-Based Principals Have a Moral Compass

- Act with Integrity
- Act Fairly
- Act Ethically
- Act Legally

Individual and Group Reflective Questions:

1. Why would Ms. Brick send the same message three times?

2. Was there anything usual about the three "NO!" messages, or were the teachers overreacting?

3. Some teachers think Ms. Brick is overstressed and possibly losing her self-control. What, if any, diplomatic way could they address the situation with her or others?

4. If Ms. Brick responds volatilely how should the teachers react?

5. What other ways/things could the teachers do to improve the campus culture and climate since Ms. Brick sees nothing wrong with it at all.

■ CASE STUDY 2: WHAT JOB?

Teachers at Carmen High School are blessed to have several fully certified teachers serving as paraprofessionals on their staff due to a lack of available teaching positions. One spring, a posting was made for which several of the certified paraprofessionals were eligible, but it was posted in such a manner that if you did not know it was there, you would not see it. In other words, it was not clearly posted for the entire community to see much less employee's right there at the school or outsiders.

Somehow, only one certified paraprofessional had inside knowledge of where to look for the posting. She applied and was given the job with no campus input. Needless to say, this did nothing positive for the campus climate or culture nor did it make the now new teacher the most popular person on campus. There was strong resentment from the other certified paraprofessionals as well as other community members who heard about it and who would have liked the opportunity to apply for the position. This made the faculty and community strongly curious of the principal's knowledge of legal and ethical issues affecting education.

Individual and Group Reflective Questions:

1. Was this posting legal?

2. Was it ethical?

3. Do the potential applicants who would have applied have a right to feel they were grieved in the way the situation was handled, or was it their responsibility to dig for postings beyond the traditional manners?

4. What should the principal do, if anything, about this situation?

5. What should the central office do, if anything, about this situation?

Figure 5.2   Ideal Principals Are Advocates for All Children

CASE STUDY 3: THERE'S A PLACE FOR EVERYONE AT OUR SCHOOL—IN SPECIAL EDUCATION ■

Juan Martinez Elementary School has a high count of English Language Learners (ELLs) but also very high scores on state accountability tests. While high scores are certainly the goal, due to the demographics, they eventually raised eyebrows with both the district and the state.

No one likes to raise eyebrows with the state.

In conducting an audit, it was determined that an indiscriminate number of ELLs were being placed in special education for no reason other than not being completely verbal in the English language. Not being verbal in the English language is not a handicapping condition for special education. The campus was placed under review and significant sanctions, including the retesting of students, were put into play. Obviously, originally the school leadership had no regard for applying legal guidelines (e.g., in relation to students with disabilities, bilingual education, confidentiality, discrimination) to protect the rights of students and staff and to improve learning opportunities.

Individual and Group Reflective Questions:

1. What is wrong with placing ELL learners in special education?

2. If the students were not verbal in English, what procedures should have been followed with what potential outcome?

3. Who would be the persons responsible for this scenario and its ramifications?

4. What is the role of the parents, if any, in this scenario?

5. What long-term legal ramifications could present themselves?

■ PRACTICE COMPETENCY QUESTIONS

1. Mrs. Mandel is concerned about a teacher, Mrs. Jackson. Ms. Jackson's ability to work with disabled and non-English speaking students is an issue. Which ethical, legal, and fair considerations should Mrs. Mandel make in relation to decisions regarding these students and the teacher?

    I. Place Mrs. Jackson on a growth improvement plan due to her inability to control her classroom

    II. Individualize professional development for Mrs. Jackson regarding special education and ELL students

    III. Terminate Mrs. Jackson due to her inability to work with students who have disabilities or have limited English proficiency

    IV. Have a conference with Mrs. Jackson to discuss students' Individualized Educational Plans and other measures

    A. I and III

    B. III only

    C. I and II

    D. II and IV

The correct answer is D.

2. After attempting to adapt to her campus culture and climate and not being successful, teacher Amanda Kutcher decides in February to abruptly resign, leaving the school in a bind. Ms. Cole, the principal, conferences with her regarding the terms of her contract, the ethics of such an abrupt departure, and what her resignation could possibly mean for her certification in the state of Texas. By doing this, Ms. Cole demonstrates her

    A. need to keep a certified teacher in the classroom.

    B. knowledge of laws regarding contracts.

    C. desire to keep Ms. Kutcher so the teacher turnover rate is low.

    D. ability to influence decisions made by her faculty.

The correct answer is B.

3. The superintendent has asked principals to implement professional learning communities at each campus. The middle school principal is concerned because some of the staff members' relationships have not been amiable lately. The seventh-grade team leader voices her opinion frequently and stirs conflict amongst teachers. Which beginning actions should the principal take?

   I. Send an e-mail asking for volunteers for a PLC committee

   II. Call a grade level leader meeting, and brainstorm ideas to start the PLC initiative and the importance of the ethics of collaboration

   III. Call a faculty meeting to give staff a heads up on the upcoming PLCs

   IV. Call a team leader meeting with the sixth-grade and eighth-grade team leaders to discuss an implementation model

   A. I and III

   B. II only

   C. II and III

   D. IV only

The correct answer is B.

4. Ms. Dahlstrom is the new principal of a Title I elementary campus. When she arrives she begins observing and investigating current operations. She notices that the sixth-grade elective music class has very few minority students. She finds out that the sixth-grade teachers have established a system in which they determine who is allowed to attend music. What should she do first?

   I. Visit with sixth-grade teachers, and listen to their reasoning for making the decisions they have made

   II. Evaluate the master schedule, and determine which classes the minority students are being placed in and why

   III. Trust the sixth-grade teachers that they are doing what is best for kids, and move on to solve other problems

   IV. Immediately adjust the master schedule, and move all sixth-grade students into music classes.

   A. III only

   B. I and II

   C. II and IV

   D. IV only

The correct answer is B.

5. The principal, Mr. Schaefer, has received a transfer request from a student at another elementary school within the district. The reason for the request states the student feels bullied by teachers and students at his current school. What should Mr. Schaefer do first?

    I. Phone the current principal to discuss the transfer request and learn more about the situation.

   II. Deny the transfer request because obviously the student will be a problem for students and staff here too

  III. Phone the parents, and find out what exactly what the problems are at the current school and why they feel they would be better here

  IV. Accept the transfer because he knows his staff is better, and the student will not have those same problems at his school

  A. II only

  B. I and III

  C. II and IV

  D. IV only

The correct answer is B.

SECTION III

DOMAIN II: INSTRUCTIONAL LEADERSHIP

6

Competency 004

Curriculum and Instruction: The Meat and Potatoes of Education

> **Key Concepts: Curriculum, Instruction, Staff Evaluation, and Development**
>
> **Competency 004:** *The principal knows how to facilitate the design and implementation of curricula and strategic plans that enhance teaching and learning; ensure alignment of curriculum, instruction, resources, and assessment; and promote the use of varied assessments to measure student performance.*

■ CASE STUDY 1: THE WIND IS NOT BENEATH HER WINGS

Harold Baldwin, principal of Rubicon High School, is faced with a situation he has not been faced with before. He has a teacher who virtually refuses to follow an Individualized Educational Plan (IEP) for a student. The teacher, Mrs. McEwen, seriously feels that modifying the curriculum and the assessment for a student weakens the standards and expectations for all students. Mr. Baldwin and Mrs. McEwen have had several conferences on the subject, but nothing has changed. She is committed to her feeling that to modify instruction and assessment would weaken the expectations for that student and, thus, be unfair to the rest of the students. She says this type of behavior has led to students graduating who cannot read and write properly, something she is strongly against. Mr. Baldwin is equally committed to promoting the use of varied assessments to measure student performance. He is also aware of the legal requirements for him to facilitate effective campus curriculum planning based on knowledge of various factors (e.g. emerging issues, occupational and economic trends, demographic data, student learning data, motivation data, motivation theory, teaching and learning theory, principles of curriculum design, human developmental processes, and legal requirements) including those written into an IEP. Thus, he and Mrs. McEwen have reached a standstill.

Individual and Group Reflective Questions:

1. What are the legal requirements of an IEP?

2. Based on the legal requirements of an IEP, does what Mrs. McEwen prefers actually matter?

3. How should Mr. Baldwin handle the situation with Mrs. McEwen?

4. Other teachers are watching the scenario unfold. Some agree with Mrs. McEwen. How should Mr. Baldwin handle the greater picture from a staff development perspective?

5. Develop a staff development plan for Rubicon based on individualized instruction and assessment.

Figure 6.1   Standards-Based Principals Provide Leadership

Competency-Based Principals Provide Leadership:

• Promote a Positive School Culture

• Provide an Effective Instructional Program

• Apply Best Practices for Student Learning

• Design Comprehensive Professional Growth Plans

CASE STUDY 2:   ■
PRETTY PITIFUL ELEMENTARY

Pretty Pitiful Elementary is a low-performing school where the teachers do not truly believe that all students can learn. First, they are not are not committed to their students having the capacity to learn and, second, they are not committed to designing and implementing new curriculum modifications, instructional strategies to improve teaching and learning, or varied assessments to measure student learning. In fact, the principal is not certain they even know how to design new curriculum modifications or to implement improved instructional strategies. He is concerned his faculty is so "old school" that they do not even understand the value of designing and implementing curricula and strategic plans that enhance teaching and learning. They are satisfied with doing the same things they've always done and expect the students to learn accordingly.

Figure 6.2 How Are We Measuring Student Learning to Ensure Educational Accountability?

Individual and Group Reflective Questions:

1. Will the students modify their learning style optimally to meet the teachers' teaching style?

2. Develop a plan where teachers learn the value of meeting individual student needs.

3. Assemble a staff development program that will introduce reluctant teachers to varied teaching and assessment techniques.

4. What should the principal do if any teachers refuse to participate in the professional development?

5. What types of professional development activities should the principal participate in so the teachers can see him modeling lifelong learning on these issues?

■ CASE STUDY 3: DOES EVERYTHING GO TOGETHER?

Ms. Ardoin is the new principal at Angelo Garza Middle School. She learned in college about the alignment of student needs with everything else, for example, staff development, curriculum, instruction, assessment, and budget development. What she does not really know is how to do these things. How does she align everything to the needs of the students to enhance student performance? It sounded so easy on paper, but now that she has to do it, she is perplexed. She remembers data being important to the process but not exactly what to look at or what to do with it.

Individual and Group Reflective Questions:

1. Why are data important to the alignment process?

2. What data should Ms. Ardoin look at first?

3. Design a model staff development process aligned with student needs.

4. Create a vision statement and goals aligned with the campus needs.

5. Generate a process for developing a budget aligned with student needs.

PRACTICE COMPETENCY QUESTIONS ■

1. A faculty meeting is held the month before the State of Texas Assessments of Academic Readiness (STAAR) exam. Your campus missed Annual Yearly Progress (AYP) the year before. The principal is emphasizing the importance of meeting the No Child Left Behind (NCLB) requirements. What will happen if your campus fails to meet AYP again?

   A. The state will require your campus to have all teachers attend a mandatory staff development on strategies for passing the STAAR test.

   B. The district will create a new curriculum for your campus.

   C. Your campus must create a new campus improvement plan.

   D. Teachers from campuses that met AYP will be moved to your campus.

The correct answer is C.

2. Ms. Lacey is the new principal at Thomas Jefferson High School. Jefferson is a large high school with a very diverse population. Upon taking the job, she was told that the campus has had some testing irregularities in the past. She decides to research this by interviewing assistant principals, counselors, and the testing coordinator. Ms. Lacey is informed by her testing coordinator that there, indeed, have been breaches in security. During the administration of the Algebra 1 end-of-course exam, a student was caught taking pictures of the test with his cell phone. Which is the appropriate state agency that should be contacted first?

   A. State Board of Education (SBOE)

   B. Texas Education Agency (TEA)

   C. State Board for Educator Certification (SBEC)

   D. Education Service Center (ESC)

The correct answer is B.

3. In the past few months, the textbook committee team adopted a new math series for the upcoming year. This is an important change since the math curriculum will be changing and many Texas Essential Knowledge and Skills (TEKS) will be moving downward. Many of the teachers have already expressed concern because they will be teaching concepts they have never taught in the past. What is the best way for the principal to best facilitate and support the changes and make this a smooth transition?

   A. Meet with individual teachers and teams to encourage them

   B. Ensure that all the teachers receive the new textbook, textbook resources, and the teacher's edition

   C. Provide training and time for teams to collaborate and discuss teaching the new concepts

   D. Ask the district coordinator to provide support

The answer is C.

4. A teacher threatens to disallow a disruptive student, Corey, back in her classroom until he is moved to another class. The principal, Ms. Sandifer, knows her first step before placing Corey in another class must be to

   A. call Corey's parents to gain permission to change his teacher to Mr. Henry, a third-year containment teacher who is passionate about special education students.

   B. call for an ARD (action, review, dismissal) meeting so the committee can make a determination as to Corey's best educational placement.

   C. call the counselor to have his or her office change Corey's status from general education to containment given his recent behavior change.

   D. talk to Corey about what he wants to do regarding being placed in a different class, then do as he wishes.

The correct answer is B.

5. Janice Jones, the principal at Thomas Edison Middle School, observes teachers focusing on students that are performing just above or below the state's proficiency level. These are often referred to as "bubble students." Teachers are directing individualized instruction specifically to these students and not to others who are performing significantly higher or lower in comparison to the "bubble students." What should she tell these teachers?

   A. They are doing a good job with the "bubble students" and need to continue their focus on them.

   B. All students can learn, thus, they need to focus on all the students.

   C. Send all the "bubble students" to content mastery so they can receive small group instruction.

   D. Allow the students who are far below the standard to be moved into a special classroom to help with specialized instruction.

The correct answer is B.

7

Competency 005

Professional Development—Student Learning
One of These Things Leads to the Other

Key Concepts: Curriculum, Instruction,
Staff Evaluation, and Development

Competency 005: *The principal knows how to advocate, nurture, and sustain an instructional program and a campus culture that are conducive to student learning and staff professional growth.*

CASE STUDY 1: IN PURSUIT ■
OF A WELL-ROUNDED PROGRAM

The principal, faculty, and staff at Pebble Brooke Intermediate are relatively satisfied with their academic program. Their students are performing well on state standardized tests, and their teachers are actively engaged in making learning interactive and personalized.

They are concerned that their programs may be lacking in the development, implementation, evaluation, and refinement of student services and activity programs to fulfill developmental, social, and cultural needs of the students. They are looking at ways to address these issues in a timely fashion.

Individual and Group Reflective Questions:

1. If the students are performing well on state exams, why does the rest matter?

2. Have schools reached the point of needing to be all things to all people? Explain your answer.

3. How should Pebble Brooke create a model to meet student developmental needs? Create an example.

4. How should Pebble Brooke create a model to meet student social needs? Create an example.

5. How should Pebble Brooke create a model to meet student cultural needs? Create an example

Figure 7.1   Identifying Campus Strengths, Weaknesses, and Trends

Low Scores ————————————————→ Areas of Weakness
High Scores ————————————————→ Areas of Strength
Moving Scores ————————————————→ Potential Trends

■ CASE STUDY 2: THE TEACHER FROM HADES

Mr. Glasscock, principal of Shamrock High School, has a math teacher, Mr. Prejean, who is not just bad, he is really bad. He does not individualize to meet the needs of the students at all. He is not friendly with students or parents. He does not attend any night programs with the community and feigns illness whenever there is an all-school program or endeavor that deviates from a traditional school day. He has been known to say mean things to students but always has a rationalization such that it can never be proven. Mr. Glasscock has met with Mr. Prejean about his attitude and teaching style several times to no avail and is quite frustrated. Mr. Prejean has been with the school 5 years and is on a continuing contract that occurred before Mr. Glasscock became principal. He is aware that the methods he is currently using with Mr. Prejean to help him advocate, nurture, and sustain an instructional program and a campus culture that are conducive to student learning and personal professional growth are not working.

Individual and Group Reflective Questions:

1. What is the root problem with Mr. Prejean's classroom demeanor?

2. What are the initial steps Mr. Glasscock should take to address this problem?

3. How can Mr. Prejean be convinced of the importance of advocating, nurturing, and sustaining an instructional program and a campus culture that are conductive to student learning and personal professional growth when he obviously does not believe in any of it?

4. Create a model growth plan for Mr. Prejean.

5. Keeping in mind Mr. Prejean's contract level, after time goes by, if the professional development plan does not work, what should Mr. Glasscock do next?

Figure 7.2   Principals as Contemporary Cultural Anthropologists

Competency-Based Principals Serve as Sociologists, Linguistics, Legal Experts, and Contemporary Cultural Anthropologists by:

- Understanding Contexts
- Responding to Contexts
- Influencing Contexts

CASE STUDY 3: FORMATIVE ■ AND SUMMATIVE *WHAT?*

Mr. Glasscock is also aware that teachers across the campus are not using formative and summative student assessment data in an appropriate manner to develop, support, and improve campus instructional strategies and goals. While the campus does have a vision statement and goals and strategies to support it, it is with the formative and summative data that the plan falls apart even with the best of the teachers. Mr. Glasscock is aware that staff development is needed in this area to best perpetuate student learning.

Individual and Group Reflective Questions:

1. Explain the difference between formative and summative assessment and why both are necessary and important.

2. Develop a model staff development program on formative and summative assessment that uses actual data.

3. How can formative assessment be used to enhance student performance. Provide an example.

4. How can summative assessment be used in a cyclical manner for the next learning cycle?

■ PRACTICE COMPETENCY QUESTIONS

1. What are some critical elements that should be included when planning curriculum?

    I. The curriculum demonstrates and recognizes the different levels of learners and diversity in the classroom.

    II. The curriculum supports all basic fundamentals of the subject.

    III. The subject/class schedule progresses in logical order.

    IV. The curriculum is in English.

    A. I, IV

    B. II, III

    C. I, II, and III

    D. I, III, and IV

The correct answer is C.

2. Mrs. Barnard is the new principal of Franklin Intermediate School, which has low reading ratings. She has decided to create a document for all the teachers to record the reading testing scores that they do three times per school year. After each class has been tested and then recorded on the document Mrs. Barnard, the teacher, and the reading specialist have a data meeting. What is the purpose of this meeting?

    A. Documentation will respond to the diverse needs on the campus.

    B. Data help to establish procedures to assess reading growth.

    C. Provide opportunities for parents to be involved in education.

    D. Looking at the data collected will help apply knowledge to issues in education.

The correct answer is B.

3. After many walk-throughs, Mr. Lewis notices that all of his teachers, except one, are using the Instructional Models for which extensive training was given at in-service. The one teacher, Mrs. Jones, has been teaching for 30 years and has great success in her classroom. Which of the following should Mr. Lewis do?

   A. Address the instructional models at staff meetings until every teacher is using them

   B. Nothing—the teacher is having great success in her classroom

   C. Meet with the teacher and discuss the models and their importance and explain that every teacher is expected to use them

   D. Recommend the teacher be terminated for noncompliance

The correct answer is C.

4. The math department has scheduled morning and afternoon tutorials to review for the upcoming State of Texas Assessments of Academic Readiness (STAAR) Algebra I end-of-course exams. A parent is complaining about the tutorial program. How should the principal handle the complaints?

   A. Have the parent set up a conference with the teachers in charge of the program.

   B. Emphasize to the parent that the tutorial program is in the best interest of his or her child.

   C. Tell the parent that his or her child does not have to attend if the child does not want to

   D. Listen to the parent's concerns, emphasize that the tutorial program will help students meet the state standards, and, thus, pass the end-of-course exams.

The correct answer is D.

5. While looking at the test scores, Ms. Arceneaux notices that the Hispanic students scored lower than the other students. As she collaborates with her team, they realize that the P-16 Initiative in Texas is a system they could use to

   I. improve teacher development.

   II. fix the salaries of teachers.

   III. close the achievement gap among ethnicities.

   IV. implement federal funded tutors.

   A. I and II

   B. III and IV

   C. I and III

   D. II and III

The correct answer is C.

8

Competency 006

Staff Evaluation: Doing It Right

Key Concepts: Curriculum, Instruction, Staff Evaluation, and Development

Competency 006: *The principal knows how to implement a staff evaluation and development system to improve the performance of all staff members, select and implement appropriate models for supervision and staff development, and apply the legal requirement for personnel management.*

■ CASE STUDY 1: WHY ARE YOU ALWAYS PICKING ON ME?

Ms. Sanderson, principal of Thomas Jefferson High School, spends considerable time doing official observations in classrooms as well as walk-throughs. She does the walk-throughs in a systematic fashion. However, one struggling teacher, Mrs. Campbell, accuses her of spending a profuse amount of time in her classroom as compared to the other classrooms. She says Ms. Sanderson is, thus, picking on her and finding fault with everything she does. Ms. Sanderson, on the other hand, says she is not spending any more time in Mrs. Campbell's room than she is anyone else's. She also says that the things she points out to Mrs. Campbell are things she would point out to any teacher. Ms. Sanderson says she is implementing a staff evaluation and development system to improve the performance of all staff members.

Individual and Group Reflective Questions:

1. Is Ms. Sanderson picking on Mrs. Campbell? Why, or why not?

2. Since Mrs. Campbell is concerned that she is being picked on, can the mentoring relationship flourish?

3. How can Ms. Sanderson improve her relationship with Mrs. Campbell? What steps must she take?

4. Given the circumstances, what is the best pathway to building a cohesive and effective growth plan for Mrs. Campbell?

5. How can a professional development plan be assisted or measured without Mrs. Campbell further feeling picked on?

Figure 8.1 For a Campus to Be Effective, Everything Must Be Perfectly Aligned

CASE STUDY 2: ANYTHING YOU CAN DO, I CAN DO BETTER

At Bloomsdale Primary School, Principal Roy Hurst is having a hard time with teacher Pamela Tolstoy. She thinks she is better than everyone else in every way including teaching techniques. She interrupts discussions at faculty meetings to tell the other teachers how they should be employing specific strategies in their classrooms, most of which are either not research based or not learner centered. She tells teachers in the workroom how they should be doing things. In fact, she will tell anyone anywhere how they should be doing things! After all, she has been teaching the same grade in the same room for 23 years!

Regretfully for all her bravado, her own ways are not perfect. Her scores are less than stellar, and her classroom discipline leaves something to be desired. She does not always individualize, and she openly admits she does not like having English Language Learners (ELLs) in her classroom. Still, her nose stays firmly planted in the air. Her attitude is having an impact on the whole school as other teachers avoid her. Mr. Hurst knows he must implement a staff evaluation and development system to improve the performance of all staff members, including Ms. Tolstoy, but he is having a difficult time dealing with her attitude.

Individual and Group Reflective Questions:

1. Attitude is a difficult thing to change. What could you do about addressing and changing this with Ms. Tolstoy?

2. Sometimes facts in black and white can speak louder than words. How can Mr. Hurst use data to give Ms. Tolstoy a reality check?

3. Ms. Tolstoy blows off the data showing her test scores being less than what they should be. She justifies the low scores with excuses such as some of her best students had the measles. How should Mr. Hurst proceed?

4. Develop a professional development plan for Ms. Tolstoy.

5. Is there ever a polite and professional way for Mr. Hurst to tell Ms. Tolstoy to get a grip, stop bullying, focus on the needs of her students, and to work collaboratively with the rest of the campus?

Figure 8.2   Vision-Goal-Daily Activities Alignment

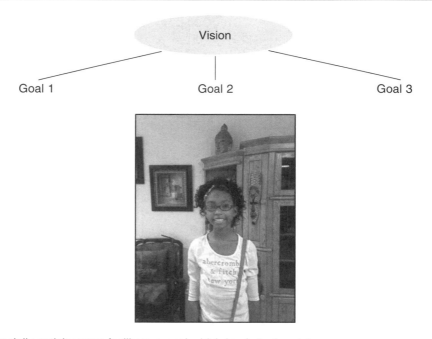

Every daily activity must facilitate a goal which leads to the vision.

CASE STUDY 3: LEADERSHIP STYLE   ■

Attila the Hun versus the Iron Hand With the Velvet Glove

After 20 years, Gilbert Middle School's beloved principal, Mr. Parr, has retired. Mr. Parr was a classic example of someone who got everything done but in a nice way. He was the iron hand with the velvet glove. He always had a kind word for everyone, even when providing less than pleasing feedback.

He has been replaced with Mr. Harris, who governs with just the iron hand and nothing from the velvet glove. He is not collaborative, believes in an authoritarian style of leadership, and does not believe in nurturing or mentoring. In fact, he has been overheard to say, "It is my way or the highway."

Faculty and staff are afraid of him. Whereas they felt they could go to Mr. Parr with anything, they never go to Mr. Harris for fear that whatever they tell him will be used against them. He does not seem to care at all about the organizational health of the campus or implementing strategies to provide ongoing support to the campus staff.

Individual and Group Reflective Questions:

1. At first glance, does Mr. Harris appear to have the attributes of an effective principal? Why, or why not?

2. What are the most effective characteristics of an effective principal?

3. What options do the teachers have to help Mr. Harris see a need to change?

4. Why is it important for the principal to implement strategies to provide ongoing support to the staff?

5. Once convinced, generate strategies Mr. Harris could use to provide ongoing support to the campus staff.

PRACTICE COMPETENCY QUESTIONS   ■

1. Mr. Hinojosa is an elementary principal who has recently left one school to take a principal position at another. He left school A with 3 weeks left in the school year. The new principal hired to take his place, Ms. Watson, discovers that Mr. Hinojosa did not finish his final teacher evaluation for Ms. Jones. She has read that it is school policy that teachers should be evaluated each year and receive feedback from the campus principal. With less than 3 weeks remaining in the school year, what should Ms. Watson do?

   A. Communicate with Ms. Jones about the situation, and schedule a time to come in and evaluate her classroom instruction

   B. Use last year's evaluation, and copy the data from it

   C. Contact the school administrative office for directions

   D. Knowing she is new to the district and coming into a difficult situation, simply ignore the lack of evaluation, and give Ms. Jones a fresh start leading into next school year

The correct answer is C.

2. Mr. Campbell is a first year Algebra 1 teacher at a Title I school. His lessons are interactive, but 60% of his students lack understanding. Every day in the teacher lounge, Mr. Campbell has been hearing rumors about the possibility of the school replacing math teachers if there are no improvements in scores. He is considering a different approach on how to enable his students to grasp the concepts of the rigorous curriculum. As Mr. Campbell's principal, you can best facilitate and support implementation of Mr. Daniels instruction by

    I.   allocating resources and materials.

    II. telling him he needs to significantly improve.

    III. providing immediate feedback on instructional methods and techniques.

    IV. using data to focus attention on improving the curriculum, instruction, and staff development.

    A. I and II

    B. II only

    C. IV and I

    D. I, III, and IV

The correct answer is D.

3. After attempting to implement Professional Learning Communities (PLC) in the school fails, what is the principal's next step?

    A. Call a faculty meeting where teachers will discuss why the program failed

    B. Ask teachers to come to a consensus regarding PLC meeting times, agendas, and student work to be addressed

    C. Create a team of teachers to plan staff development on PLCs for the teachers and staff

    D. Wait until the teachers are more interested

The correct answer is C.

4. Cumberland High School is having significant teacher turnover on the campus. This year, the assistant principal has requested a transfer to another campus within the district. Teacher absences have increased, and they are bickering among each other. Mr. Washington presents at all campus professional development trainings and leads faculty meetings in an authoritarian manner. He encourages teachers to participate in the decision-making process but ultimately makes the decisions in all cases. After receiving the monthly teacher attendance report and the teacher transfer request list, Mr. Washington realizes that he needs to address these issues. He should address these issues by

I. taking a strong introspective look at himself for his strengths and weaknesses.

II. creating and sending out an anonymous survey with campus morale questions and short answers to help him improve.

III. denying all teacher transfers.

IV. encouraging all teachers to present on topics at campus professional development meetings, faculty meeting, and use their input for all professional development.

A. III and IV

B. I, II, and IV

C. II and IV

D. I and III

The correct answer is B.

5. Mr. Washington contacts the educational service center to seek professional development training on leadership mentoring for him and several of the teachers. He has enough money budgeted to pay for a total of six people. When selecting teachers who could best benefit from this training, Mr. Washington should consider

I. any teacher on a growth plan.

II. all grade level teacher leaders.

III. new teachers.

IV. any interested teacher who exhibits leadership potential and selfless qualities.

A. I and IV

B. II and IV

C. III and IV

D. I and II

The correct answer is B.

9

Competency 007

Making Sound Data-Based Decisions:
Easier Said Than Done

> **Key Concepts: Curriculum, Instruction,**
> **Staff Evaluation, and Development**
>
> **Competency 007:** *The principal knows how to apply organizational, decision-making, and problem-solving skills to ensure an effective learning environment.*

■ CASE STUDY 1: BUSY WORK PRINCIPAL

Mr. Henderson at Rollin High School is so obsessed with documentation that he has the teachers buried in paperwork. It has reached the point that they cannot spend adequate time collaborating and planning appropriate instructional strategies per student because they are swamped with time-consuming redundant paperwork. Several of the senior teachers have approached Mr. Henderson to ask him to back off the paperwork a little bit, but he is adamant that it is necessary in case the Texas Education Agency (TEA) ever does an audit of the campus. Frustration is running very high. Teachers feel Mr. Henderson needs significant improvement in implementing appropriate management techniques and group process skills to define roles, assign functions, delegate authority, and determine accountability for campus goal attainment.

Individual and Group Reflective Questions:

1. Is there a point of diminishing productivity and return regarding paperwork? If so, how can that point be determined?

2. How should Mr. Henderson balance required and nonrequired paperwork with teacher frustration?

3. How can it be determined how much documentation really is necessary in case of a TEA audit?

4. Formulate a model where Mr. Henderson could define and delegate certain functions and roles such that everyone does not have to do everything compliance related.

5. Construct an accountability system with a timeline to ensure everything gets done in an accurate and timely manner without killing all the staff.

Figure 9.1   Collaborative Data-Based Decision Making Is Necessary to Achieve a Student-Focused Campus Vision

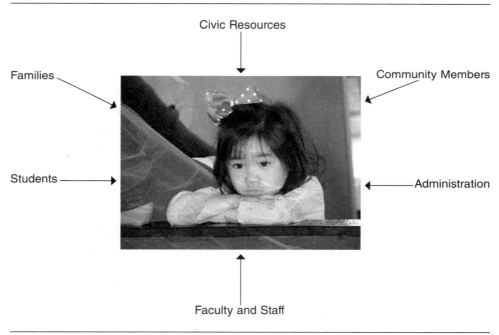

CASE STUDY 2: CAN'T ORGANIZE SQUAT   ■

Tamara Ylimaki, the new principal of Orange Orchard Elementary, appears to have significant organizational issues. She wants to make changes to the way things have been done in the past but has sought no collaboration to the change process regarding the fundamental ways the school is structured. She remembers being taught to encourage and facilitate positive change, enlist support for change, and overcome obstacles to change, yet 2 days before school starts the master schedule is still not in place. Special programs such as physical education, music, art, and lunch have not been integrated into the schedule. New enrollees have not been assigned to classes. Textbooks have not been distributed, and teachers are close to hysterical while trying to keep up a false calm to parents and community members that, yes, school is indeed starting in 2 days. Ms. Ylimaki appears to be attempting to do everything herself while not incorporating the campus in the changes taking place regarding the basic organization of students.

Individual and Group Reflective Questions:

1. Describe a model change process on any topic.

2. How can Ms. Ylimaki calm the faculty and staff down?

3. Create a collaborative model Ms. Ylimaki could use to involve others in decision making regarding getting the remaining essential projects done and communicated.

4. Should, or how should, parents be involved in these endeavors?

5. Construct a model assessment system to ensure all endeavors are done with quality and on time.

Figure 9.2   Using Data to Improve the Process for Greater Student Achievement

Enhancing Education = Making Lives Better.

■   CASE STUDY 3: WHO CAN GET TO HIM LAST?

Thomas Rhodes, the new principal at Bergman Elementary, is so collegial that he wanted to make everyone happy. Teachers soon learned that if they had an idea on something, it was not a matter of getting to him first to persuade him their idea was a good one. He would agree with anything they said anyway.

They key was to get to him last. If there was more than one view on a topic, they knew not to attempt to approach him first. They tried to approach him last because the person that got to him last was the one whose idea stuck. If you got to him last, no one else could attempt to change his mind. This, of course, created great confusion and frustration among the prior people he had previously said yes to. Thus, confusion and frustration reigned. Mr. Rhodes needed help in knowing how to apply organizational, decision-making, and problem-solving skills to ensure an effective learning environment. Remember, be last!

Individual and Group Reflective Questions:

1. How can Mr. Rhodes be approached regarding his decision-making strategies not working without making him angry?

2. What traits would cause Mr. Rhodes to constantly change his mind and always go with the last idea presented to him?

3. What, if anything, can be done about Mr. Rhodes poor decision-making skills?

4. Develop a professional growth plan to help Mr. Rhodes break this negative and counterproductive habit.

5. If none of this works, what recourse should the teachers take?

PRACTICE COMPETENCY QUESTIONS ■

1. A well-loved and knowledgeable teacher has a serious complaint filed against him by a student and parent. The teacher has no record of any infractions and has high success rates from his students. Because of the timing of the incident, the teacher is replaced with a degreed, but not certified, long-term sub. Students' grades are starting to drop, and parents are beginning to ask questions. What is the best course of action for the principal to take in order to address the situation with parents?

   A. Write a letter explaining to parents that there is a substitute in the room that will be there until the end of the year

   B. Send an e-mail to all parents explaining that there is a noncertified long-term sub in the class to finish the year

   C. Send a letter home with the students explaining the situation and inviting parents to a "coffee with the principal" where the parents can come to ask questions about the new teacher situation

   D. Do not address the situation with the parents, but send the science instructional coach into that class to assist the substitute with teaching the curriculum

The correct answer is C.

2. The new principal, Jonas Garza, starts an initiative to change the culture of the school. He changes the colors in the hallway, enacts new curriculum in the science classes, and makes other unsolicited changes. After 6 weeks, a number of faculty complaints arise. Which of the following is the most appropriate statement regarding the situation?

A. He acted according to the position he was hired for and is justified in his actions.

B. He has not gone far enough and needs to enact curriculum changes for all core subjects and change the method for submitting lesson plans.

C. He should adhere to all district mandates and regulations when enacting change, while also garnering input from all stakeholders in the district.

D. He should rewrite the mission and goals of the school on a whim to enact his personal beliefs onto the district policies.

The correct answer is C.

3. Principal Sara Blandford is in the middle of an action, review, and dismissal (ARD) meeting when she receives an urgent text asking her to come to the front office immediately. What should she do?

A. Stay in the ARD meeting because an administrator is required to attend and ask her assistant principal to handle the issue in the front office

B. Leave the ARD meeting because the text is from a parent who is a friend of hers, and the ARD team already knows the services that will be provided to the student

C. Immediately call the assistant principal to finish the ARD so she can deal with the unexpected issue

D. Halt the ARD, and ask the diagnostician to find another date

The correct answer is C.

4. The principal meets with the fourth-grade math teachers to address the poor results on the second benchmark assessment. Which items below should the principal request teachers bring to have the most meaningful discussion?

I. Benchmark #2 assessments with Texas Essential Knowledge and Skills (TEK) and socioeconomic breakdown

II. Student music, art, and PE grades

III. Benchmark #1 data with student TEK and socioeconomic breakdown results

IV. Student reading benchmark results

A. I and IV

B. I, III, and IV

C. II and IV

D. I and III

The correct answer is B.

5. What course of action should the principal take to follow up the meeting with the fourth-grade math teachers?

    I. Create a plan, and adjust daily instruction based on the student data studied

    II. Visit the fourth-grade math teachers during instruction and share his or her observations with individual teachers regarding their instructional practices

    III. Establish a timeline of future meeting to continue analyzing the data and prepare for the next benchmark assessment

    IV. None of the above

    A. I and II

    B. I and III

    C. I, II, and III

    D. IV

The correct answer is C.

SECTION IV

DOMAIN III: ADMINISTRATIVE LEADERSHIP

10

Competency 008

Campus Management at Its Finest

Key Concepts: Budget, Student Safety, Facilities

Competency 008: *The principal knows how to apply principles of effective leadership and management in relation to campus budgeting, personnel, resource utilization, financial management, and technology use.*

■ CASE STUDY 1: BUDGET DEVELOPMENT

The principal, Maynard Bratlien, and assistant principal, Conrad Monk, of Thomas Edison Middle School, are in disagreement as to how to develop the following year's budget. Mr. Monk thinks the easiest way to do it would be to look at how much was spent in each category the previous year and adjust accordingly. Mr. Bratlien feels the budget should be a collaborative endeavor built by the teachers and based on the needs of the students as determined by data analysis. Mr. Monk feels that, in the end, it will all wash out close to the same. Since everyone is incredibly busy, why take the extra time to involve the teachers with all that data analysis?

Individual and Group Reflective Questions:

1. Is one of the forms of budget development preferable over the other? Why, or why not?

2. Will the difference in the process or the product of budget development "all wash out?" Why, or why not?

3. Why is data analysis important to budget development and the analyzation of student needs?

4. Should, or should not, the teachers be involved in data analysis? Why, or why not?

5. Some districts strictly allocate money on a per pupil basis. From an equity perspective, what is your opinion? Support your rationale.

Figure 10.1   Competency-Based Principals as Managers

Competency-Based Principals Are Good Managers as Well as Good Leaders:

- Campus Budget
- Personnel
- Resources Utilization
- Financial Management
- Use of Technical
- Equipment

CASE STUDY 2: BUT WHY CAN'T WE . . . ? ■

With monies short in most schools and school districts, the site-based management team at John R. Hoyle High School is befuddled as to why the very healthy special education fund cannot be used in other needed areas. The way they see it, there is more money than necessary in the special education fund and not enough money virtually everywhere else. Therefore, why can't they use the special education money elsewhere? The principal has referred to the special education money as federal funds. Shouldn't the resource use of federal funds go to help all children rather than just one segment?

Individual and Group Reflective Questions:

1. Explain the concept of federal funds versus state and local, what can be used for what, and why.

2. Explain the distinctions of special education monies and why they cannot be used outside that arena.

3. Why should, or should not, special education, receive extra allocations that others cannot use?

4. There are many "fall-through-the-cracks" students who need assistance but do not qualify for special education. Their needs are

attempted to be met via Section 504 of the Americans with Disabilities Act and other programs. Can special education money be used to assist these students? Why, or why not?

5. Explain the funding, if any, for Section 504 of the Americans with Disabilities Act.

Figure 10.2   The Campus Success Flowchart

■ CASE STUDY 3: SOFTWARE UTILIZATION

A teacher attends a professional conference. While there she visits the resource booths where she finds some excellent software that she feels will be of benefit to her students. She purchases it with personal funds.

Upon her return to campus, she shows it to her principal who is equally impressed with it. He reimburses her for her purchase. Since she was reimbursed, the teacher considers the software the property of the school and shares it with her peers. She considers her sharing a part of collegial collaboration for the purpose of technology use.

Individual and Group Reflective Questions:

1. Is sharing this software legal? Why or why not?

2. Some teachers would like to make copies of the software to use in their classrooms, too. Since the school reimbursed the teacher who bought the software, would this be legal? Why, or why not?

3. The original teacher is highly satisfied with the results of the software. She has kept the company's brochure and sees more software she thinks would be helpful to her students. She approaches the

principal about the school purchasing more software for the campus. What legal and ethical considerations must be considered?

4. A parent wants to know if he can copy the software if he provides the CDs. Would this be legal or ethical? Support your answer.

5. The original teacher is chagrined that the original purchase and reimbursement has stirred up such a hornet's nest of interest, some of which is controversial. Was there anything wrong with her original purchase or reimbursement? If so, what?

PRACTICE COMPETENCY QUESTIONS ■

1. Ms. Ruffin is a first-year administrator at a high school campus. She has received many requests from teachers and support staff for various budgetary items. What would be the best practice for her to properly allocate the funds budgeted for her campus?

   A. Before beginning with the budget plan, Ms. Ruffin must start with the campus goals and vision.

   B. Ms. Ruffin should divide her budget equally among all departments in order to fairly distribute funds.

   C. Ms. Ruffin should carefully review last year's spending plan in order to know how to distribute the funds.

   D. As a first-year administrator, Ms. Ruffin should comply with all requests in order to gain acceptance among her staff.

The correct answer is A.

2. Mrs. Comeaux is a parent of a student that will be attending Southside High as a ninth grader in the fall. During the summer months, Mrs. Comeaux researches the school report card for the last 2 academic years. Her findings show that the school has not met Annual Yearly Progress (AYP) and is receiving intervention from the state. Mrs. Comeaux goes to withdraw her student from Southside but is told that this is not an option, and her student must attend. Which federal legislation is not being following?

   I. Americans With Disabilities Act (1990)

   II. No Child Left Behind Act

   III. Elementary and Secondary Education Act

   IV. Title IX

   A. I and IV

   B. II only

   C. II and III

   D. None of the above

The correct answer is B.

3. Mr. Petry, the principal of Lincoln High, recently enrolled an incoming female sophomore student who speaks very little English. Mr. Petry must make sure that the proper steps are taken to ensure the student is accommodated and receives support so that she can progress effectively through the educational system. Which law was established to ensure the success of the non-English proficient students?

    A. Americans with Disabilities Act

    B. ESL Statutes

    C. Bilingual Education Act

    D. P.L.94–142

The correct answer is C.

4. Mrs. Johansson, the parent of an 18-year-old senior at Martin High School has concerns regarding her daughter's grades. She calls the school to request a copy of them. The administration informs her that she needs consent from her daughter to review the records. What act prohibits parents and legal guardians from having access to school records once the child turns 18 or attends school beyond the high school level?

    A. No Child Left behind

    B. Family Educational Rights and Privacy Act (FERPA)

    C. Title IX

    D. Section 504 of the Americans With Disabilities Act

The correct answer is B.

5. Mr. Smith has been the principal at Lakeview Middle School for the past 10 years. Portions of the school, which was built in the late 1960s, are in need of significant repairs and technology updates. Upon the superintendent's direction to address the necessary repairs at Lakeview, Mr. Smith develops the following budgetary plan:

    1. conduct a needs assessment for each classroom in need of repair,

    2. contact local contractors in order to obtain competitive repair bid, and

    3. organize project proposal for site budgetary committee meeting.

    Mr. Smith could best improve his budgetary plan by doing which of the following?

    A. Include faculty, staff, and community members in budgetary discussions and planning for the project

    B. Hold a fundraiser event to raise money for the project

    C. Enlist the help of other local administrators to develop the budget

    D. Allocate budgetary funds from other local funds for the repairs

The correct answer is A.

11

Competency 009

*Campus and Student Safety
as Top Priorities*

Key Concepts: Budget, Student Safety, Facilities

Competency 009: *The principal knows how to apply principles of effective leadership and management to the campus physical plant and support systems to ensure a safe and effective learning environment.*

■ CASE STUDY 1: THIS IS NOT A DRILL!

A certain Friday did not turn out to be the best in the history of Blair High School. There was a fire drill that did not turn out to be a drill. However, some of the students did not take the supposed drill seriously, and a fight broke out between two rival gangs on the school yard. As campus security worked to settle it down, the city fire and police showed up because it really was not a drill. This shocked the two gangs so much that they broke the fight up themselves. After everything finally settled down, the campus team realized they had work to do on applying strategies for ensuring the safety of students and personnel and for addressing emergencies and security concerns. That day's emergency had, indeed, not gone well.

Individual and Group Reflective Questions:

1. What could have been done proactively to prevent the rival gangs from being near each other?

2. What methods could the campus have used to break up the fight before it started?

3. What ramifications should be taken against the gangs for breaking fire drill protocol much less starting a fight on campus?

4. Brainstorm strategies the campus could better apply for ensuring the safety of students and personnel and for addressing emergencies and security concerns.

5. Develop an assessment plan aligned with an emergency management plan.

■ CASE STUDY 2: POWER OUTAGE

One morning during second period at Lakeside Intermediate School, Mr. Honcho, the principal, was notified by the cafeteria of a gas leak.

Figure 11.1   Student Safety Is Paramount

The leak was immediately reported, and the students in the areas around the leak were immediately moved while the gas, fire, and police departments were notified. All classes were kept where they were. There were no transition periods. During the crisis, everyone, including teachers, stayed in a prolonged second period. Three fire trucks, a police car, and a representative from the local gas company showed up while students watched from the windows.

Due to a totally separate incident, a truck hit a large power line down the street, which also knocked out the power at the school. Now the school was without electricity and gas. Mr. Honcho could not communicate with faculty or students via the public address system because it was not working. There were five handheld communication devices that were distributed one per building in the multicampus facility. Mr. Honcho and the assistant principal consistently walked the campus for any potential problems and for communication reasons.

Throughout the entire event, which lasted several hours, the campus remained calm in large part due to Mr. Honcho's placid demeanor. Later, he joked that if anything bad could happen, it would—and obviously did. Mr. Honcho obviously knew how to implement strategies that enable the school physical plant equipment and support systems to operate safely, efficiently, and effectively even during a double emergency.

Individual and Group Reflective Questions:

1. Part of the campus was relocated due to the gas leak. Should the remaining part have been relocated too? Why, or why not?

2. What else could have been done to ensure student safety?

3. Why were the students and teachers kept in a prolonged second period?

4. What would have been the best way to notify families of the double emergency, or, was that necessary at all?

5. Create a potential assessment plan to measure the crisis management plan after the emergency was over.

CASE STUDY 3: THEY'VE ■ GOT GUNS! LOCK DOWN!

A metropolitan high school experienced high drama when persons showed up outside the school waving guns and yelling. The campus went into immediate lock down while the emergency management plan was put fully in place and the police were called. Glass interior and exterior windows were covered with paper so no one could see inside. Desks were moved against doors as well as against low lying windows. The school was on full red alert, but, thanks to practicing their emergency management plans, the calm demeanor of the administration, and the quick reaction of both the campus security and the local police department, the incident passed without anyone being hurt. The campus security team worked closely with the local police and the gun wavers were apprehended. Everyone practiced the previously developed and implemented procedures for crisis planning and for responding to crises. The practice paid off.

Figure 11.2 Turn Obstacles Into Student-Focused Learning Opportunities

It was a day to tell their families about.

Individual and Group Reflective Questions:

1. What else could campus administration have done to ensure student and staff safety?

2. What could be added to the campus crisis management plan as manifested here?

3. After the crisis was over, in what ways could the campus counselors be used?

4. After the crisis was over, what strategies could the teachers have used to calm the students down so teaching and learning could resume?

5. In truth, will any more significant learning occur late in the day after such a traumatic event?

■ PRACTICE COMPETENCY QUESTIONS

1. Christina is an outstanding student and volleyball player at the local high school in her small town. She comes from a single parent family and lives 10 miles from the school. Her mother picks cotton during the day and works in a local restaurant at night to make ends meet. After the last game of the season, Christina is the last out of the locker room only to find out that everyone except Mr. Green, the principal, has left. Further, her mother will not be available to pick her up due to car trouble. Christina asks Mr. Green for a ride home as it is too far to walk, and it is late in the evening. What should Mr. Green do?

   A. Call a female administrator or faculty member to join him on the ride to take Christina home

   B. Pick up Christina's mom before it gets dark, and come back for Christina to take them both home

   C. Take Christina home, asking her to sit in the back seat of his car, so that she doesn't feel uncomfortable

   D. Because the bus yard is near Christina's home, Mr. Green should ask a bus driver to take Christina home

The correct answer is A.

2. The principal, Ms. Dyson-Vannett, talks with a teacher regarding her propensity to put children out in the hallway unsupervised. Ms. Dyson-Vannett informs the teacher that she is unable to place students anywhere that they are not being supervised by a certified adult. This conversation shows Ms. Dyson-Vannett's knowledge regarding

   A. state laws regarding supervision.

   B. district policy regarding supervision.

   C. school procedures.

   D. personal preferences for safety.

The correct answer is A.

3. The principal has observed the assistant principal dealing with a higher percentage of bullying incidents lately and wants to address the situation. To that end, what steps could he or she take?

   I. Spend time in the hallways and cafeteria, and encourage staff to actively monitor students during lunch, recess, and transitions to decrease the undesired incidents

   II. Call the local Education Service Center, and ask them to conduct an assembly for the students on bullying prevention

   III. Establish a student-to-student mentoring program, and focus on building meaningful relationships amongst students

   IV. Monitor the situation to see if it improves on its own

A. IV

B. I and II

C. II and IV

D. I, II, and III

The correct answer is D.

4. The principal notices there are a number of students in the hallways during instructional time. Concerned, the principal brings up the subject at a faculty meeting to solve this problem. Concern is expressed both about the loss of critical instructional time and student safety. This effort addresses which of the following aspects of the principal's role?

   I. Collaboration

   II. Decision-making

   III. Analyzation

   IV. Justification

   A. I and IV

   B. II and IV

   C. IV

   D. I, II, and III

The correct answer is D.

5. Mr. Watson, the principal of Enid Intermediate School, will be leading a team in updating the school's emergency management plan so members of the school community will know what to do in case of a crisis. Which of the following is the first step to be the most useful to take in this effort?

   A. Meet with community leaders to identify individuals and resources available to assist the school in various emergencies

   B. Review the emergency plans of similar schools, and compare them to the school's current plan

   C. Solicit information from local police, fire, and public health personnel about potential school vulnerabilities and appropriate responses

   D. Research each element of the school's current crisis management plan to assess compliance with relevant laws and regulations

The correct answer is D.

SECTION V
SUMMING IT UP

12

Here a Question, There a Question, Everywhere a Question, Question

■ BRINGING IT ALL TOGETHER

So, we have been through all the domains and competencies, done 27 case studies, responded to a million open-ended higher-order thinking questions for reflection and discussion, and about a zillion decision set practice questions. Now we have come to the end of the trail.

What to Do When the Going Is Tough

What do you do if you have thoroughly read and studied my *Passing the Principal TExES Exam: Keys to Certification and School Leadership (2nd ed.)*, practiced with my practice test book, now have worked your way through this book, and you still have not passed the exam (*highly* unlikely!)

Then it is time to face the reality that your foundational knowledge is lacking, or you have a reading comprehension problem. Until you fix those issues, you will have a problem.

How do you fix them?

1. Look at your test score sheet. Find your lowest domain. That will tell you the area you need the *most* work in.

2. Go to the back of *Passing the Principal TExES Exam: Keys to Certification and School Leadership (2nd ed.).* There you will find the Suggested Additional Resources. They are divided into the three domains. Believe me, there are more there than you covered in your entire master's program, so there are plenty.

3. Go to the domain where you are the lowest. Pick at least five of those resources that you have access to and STUDY THEM. They have the foundational basis that you are lacking, so learn from them!

4. You do not need to buy every book. Borrow from friends, from your district, from your public library, or your university library. Even public libraries, which do not cater to graduate texts, will order any resource you need for free through interlibrary loan. All you need is an old fashioned library card!

5. The other thing that could be holding you back is your reading comprehension skills. It could be that you are reading the decision sets but not understanding the nuances of what they are asking you. In that case, please don't take this wrong, but ask an English teacher in your district, preferably on the middle school level, for direction. They can point you to resources that will help your reading skills. Your reading skills will improve your TExES scores, so suck up a little pride, and do what it takes to get over this hump. Besides, the improvement in your reading comprehension skills will serve you well for the rest of your life.

Some Last Reminders

If you bite the bullet and do these things, you will pass the test. Remember to think ideal. Remember your Sherrys. Remember the 1–2–3–4 Plan. Use all of them on the day you test.

Then contact me when you pass, and we will be like the Partridge Family and be "happy together!"

I have faith in you that you will knock the top out of this test the first time. That is our goal. But if it does not happen, we do not give up. We never give up. We keep on working to improve ourselves exactly like we teach our students to do every day.

And with all of that being said, let me close with a quote that I hope will guide your life:

May the Lord bless you and keep you.

May the Lord make His face to shine upon you,

And be gracious to you;

The Lord lift up His countenance upon you,

And give you peace.

Numbers 6: 24—26
New King James Version

To your future!
Elaine Wilmore

References

Reavis, G. H. (1940, 1999 reprint). *The animal school.* Peterborough, NH: Crystal Spring Books.

Wilmore, E. L. (2013). *Passing the Principal TExES Exam: Keys to Certification and School Leadership (2nd ed.).* Thousand Oaks, CA: Corwin.

Wilmore, E. L. (2015). *Passing the Principal TExES Exam: Practice Tests for Success.* Thousand Oaks, CA: Corwin.

Index

Page references followed by (figure) indicate an illustrated figure or photograph.

CORWIN
A SAGE Company

Helping educators make the greatest impact

CORWIN HAS ONE MISSION: to enhance education through intentional professional learning.

We build long-term relationships with our authors, educators, clients, and associations who partner with us to develop and continuously improve the best evidence-based practices that establish and support lifelong learning.